PRIVATE ROAD

AMS PRESS
NEW YORK

PRIVATE ROAD

by

FORREST REID

FABER AND FABER LTD
LONDON

Library of Congress Cataloging in Publication Data

Reid, Forrest, 1875-1947.
    Private road.

    Continues Apostate, the first part of the author's
autobiography.
    Reprint of the 1940 ed. published by Faber and Faber,
London.
    1. Reid, Forrest, 1875-1947—Biography. 2. Authors,
English—20th century—Biography. I. Title.
PR6035.E43Z52 1978   823'.9'12[B]   75-41225
ISBN 0-404-14587-6

124684

Reprinted from the edition of 1940, London
First AMS edition published in 1978
Manufactured in the United States of America

AMS PRESS INC.
NEW YORK, N.Y.

Dedication

When you are old your eyes by chance may light
Upon this book, and in the quiet night
Beside the drowsy fire memory may weave its
    spell.
Then shall the writer enter like a ghost
To stand beside his all unconscious host,
Summoned from dim far fields his tale to tell.

"I am half convinced that the reflection is indeed the reality, the real thing which nature imperfectly images to our grosser sense."—HAWTHORNE.

"Tant qu'il y aura des bois, des prés, des montagnes, des lacs et des rivières, tant que les blanches vapeurs du matin s'élèveront au-dessus des ruisseaux, il y aura des nymphes; il y aura des fées. Elles sont la beauté du monde: c'est pourquoi elles ne périront jamais."—ANATOLE FRANCE.

"Everywhere he carried this passion for humanizing things. . . . Inanimate nature became not merely animate, but human. The Greek could not think of rivers without their river-gods, or of sun and moon apart from their divinities. Naiads live in springs and are the authors of their clearness; Dryads are the tree-spirits that die when the tree is felled. A sudden fright seizes some shepherds as they feed their flock on the hillside; it was Pan who peered out at them from among the rocks." —R. W. LIVINGSTONE.

"Elderly persons would be utterly intolerable if they remembered *everything*. *Everything*, nevertheless, is just what they themselves would like to remember, and just what they would like to tell to *everybody*. Be sure that the Ancient Mariner, though he remembered quite as much as his audience wanted to hear, and rather more, about the albatross and the ghastly crew, was inwardly raging at the sketchiness of his own mind."— MAX BEERBOHM.

I

THIRTEEN years ago, in 1926 to be exact, I published the first part of an autobiography, which I called *Apostate*. Other people, it is true, for some unknown reason preferred to call it *The Apostate*, but that falsified my meaning, the title was intended to indicate a state of mind, not a person—the state of mind in question being for the most part nothing more alarming than the reluctance of a small boy to go to church, and his "passion for humanizing things", his pleasure in discovering river-gods, tree-spirits, and the divinities of sun and moon. *The Library* of Apollodorus would have been exactly his kind of book had he ever chanced to come across it; as it was, he had to content himself with a very dry and inadequate history of pagan mythology, which, nevertheless, at the age of nine he knew practically by heart.

Apostate was the story of this boy, and it broke off when he had reached the age of seventeen or eighteen. Of all my books perhaps it was the easiest to write. Once I had got under way, I received a more immediate and intimate pleasure from writing *Uncle Stephen;* but in *Apostate* I had nothing to change, nothing to invent, nothing to ponder. I simply watched and listened, while the whole thing was re-enacted before me. On the stage the light of the past was focused, and I sat gazing, as if from some darkened auditorium, attentive, yet directing nothing, letting the figures come and go at their own will, listening to what they said, hearing the sound of their voices, but never consciously inventing their words. Then, at a particular moment, the light was extinguished, the curtain dropped—and I knew that this part of the story was over.

True, I have to some extent followed the same method when writing a novel, but in a novel only certain individual scenes present themselves in this fashion; there is a lot to be done besides. *Apostate* was a prologue, and at the same time it was complete in itself. Could I carry it further? My publishers wanted me to, a good many readers urged me to, but, though I pretended otherwise, I myself felt little confidence. *They* didn't know, I alone knew, how much, as an author, I resembled Mr. Dick. I could get on swimmingly until I reached my King Charles's head—the point where a boy becomes a man. Then something seemed to happen, my inspiration was cut off, my interest flagged, so that all became a labour, and not a labour of love. I supposed it must be some mysterious form of arrested development. Certainly I had intended to write a sequel to *Following Darkness* for example, and had even thrown out obscure hints to this effect in the course of the book. Yet, when the time came to do it, the idea had lost its attractiveness, I felt very dubious; therefore, from the revised version, *Peter Waring*, I removed the hints, and left the story of the grown-up Peter to the reader's imagination.

In the same way I kept putting off the completion of *Apostate*. The method, I could see, would have to be quite different. In those childhood and boyhood chapters all was spontaneous, no reconstruction was necessary, because there were so few characters, so few events, and so small a corner of life had to be covered. Later the stage and happenings were crowded, selection became imperative, and a continuous narrative impossible. It was really the pattern in *Apostate* that guided me; I wrote it just as it happened, and the whole picture held together; but in the swarming years that followed I could discover no pattern. In the beginning there had been a story; at the other end I might find another story; but this I did not propose to tell, and how, at any rate, connect them? Nothing that had occurred in my boyhood was forgotten, but much that had occurred since was forgotten; and what remained was scattered and fragmentary. From time to time, like every other novelist, I had used portions of autobiographical material in the tales I was writing; but that was different, because I mixed truth freely with invention. In fact, it was only when the task had been abandoned definitely as hopeless that it struck me I might find a thread of continuity, if a very loose one, by following the composition of these tales themselves, explaining

the intention and aspiration behind them, treating
them, where I could, less as literary experiments
than as milestones on the road. For from this
point of view they were by no means equally
significant. The significant had sprung up of their
own accord, so to speak; the others were the in-
ventions of a professional writer in search of a
story to tell, and bore traces of Mr. Dick's
struggles with King Charles's head.

Such then, more or less, is the plan I have followed here. The whole should be taken as the
chronicle of a prolonged personal adventure, a
kind of pilgrim's progress viewed dispassionately
and I think without conscious prejudice. That
is why I have included certain letters, not because
they express a literary criticism favourable or
unfavourable—in either case this would be beside
the point—but because they are directly relevant
to my main subject and help to illustrate it. I
received encouragement and I received dis-
couragement and I have recorded both.

II

WE live our customary workaday life in a world fairly well known to us, because we have explored it from earliest childhood, but that world is like a tiny island in an immense sea, unknown and perhaps unknowable. By unknown I mean uncharted, since we do not question its existence; but that we shall ever comprehend its nature, its meaning or its purpose, I for one feel more than doubtful. Dreams, aspirations, ideals—these may result in faith; but faith is not knowledge, and one can have a passionate faith in an illusion.

> Still we say as we go,——
>   Strange to think by the way,
> Whatever there is to know,
>   That shall we know one day.

But why? Does Rossetti now know? Not, I think, if he is still Rossetti. One thing at all events is infinitely improbable, that the truth in the least resembles what any human being has ever imagined or any religion taught.

Yet I believe in religion, in so far as it is the symbol of an ideal. But no farther, for I also believe that the letter killeth. Man has made God —many Gods indeed—in his own image—I have made one myself. Therefore it is not surprising that these Gods should differ, since some have been conceived in fear and others in love and admiration. All are human, but that does not necessarily mean

that none is divine. And again I am speaking in
human terms, for our conception of divinity is of
a perfected humanity existing out of space, out of
time, and above all out of the body with its animal
needs and desires. What is left is a naked spiritual
energy. Yet is that God? Not the God we want,
so we re-endow him with certain human qualities
—sympathy, compassion, goodness—which may
have no existence outside our own minds.

Looking back at the remote and rather lonely
figure of the boy I wrote about in *Apostate* (far
more remote, now, than the Tom of *Uncle
Stephen* and *The Retreat*), I see him as sharing this
very general, if not universal, desire for God.
Only in his case it was *a* God, for his religious
sense was more canine than human. Perhaps he
had no religious sense at all; he was often told so;
all I can affirm is that he led two lives—one the
external life of his games, collections, and the rest
of it; the other a private life haunted by visions of
beauty and the longing for an ideal companion
who would bring him the happiness he had only
known in imagination. He was

> the wretched slave,
> Who like a lackey, from the rise to the set,
> Sweats in the eye of Phoebus, and all night
> Sleeps in Elysium.

Yet the essence of this ideal was the belief that
beauty and goodness (his sort of "goodness"—
kindness and simplicity and generosity) are inseparable. He found support for it in the teaching

of Socrates, but not in that of Saint Paul, not even
in that of the later, colder Plato. And he was not
an "intellectual"; beauty and goodness were
qualities which the moment he thought of them
became flesh. True, he "saw them in eternity", but
so also he saw the aspects of nature—trees and
rivers and the sea. All were reflections from, and
pledges of, a divine world existing beyond the
flux of time and fate and change. It was no more
divine really, I dare say, than the Fortunate
Islands, which indeed it very closely resembled.
All I mean is that he could not help believing in
it, or being haunted by it, which perhaps is not
quite the same thing, and that the vision—though
offering a refuge where he could retire and dream
happy dreams—was, in one sense, not helpful to
him. For it floated between him and the world in
which he had to make a living, colouring his
standards of success and failure, so that they
became irreconcilable with those that were con-
stantly being dinned into his ears. Counsels of
practical wisdom left him not so much recalcitrant
as indifferent, since even while they buzzed about
him, and their plausibility was apparent to common sense, he found himself turning back to
something else, as the only *real* thing. And such
a state of mind is dangerous when neither mind
nor character is mature.

> What of all the will to do?
>   It has vanished long ago.
> For a dream-shaft pierced it through
>   From the Unknown Archer's bow.

> What of all the soul to think?
>   Someone offered it a cup
> Filled with a diviner drink,
>   And the flame has burned it up.

That was the danger, for after all the practical problem was there, and he had to deal with it.

But I do not wish to exaggerate—nor, for that matter, to keep up this rather irritating affectation of the third person. Let me say then that *I* had to deal with it, and add that in many respects I felt myself perfectly competent to do so. It was merely that I found the commercial life into which I had been thrust both a bore and a blind alley. Regarded even from the most realistic point of view, it offered little chance of success, and no scope at all for such abilities and interests as I possessed. These pointed clearly to a job in a library or a museum. Working amongst books or prints, I should have been in my natural element (the Print Room of the British Museum was what I should have chosen had a choice been offered), but I had no one to advise or help me, and my mother was dead against my going to London. Doubtless if I myself had possessed more boldness and determination something might have been done. I was, however, in the practical affairs of life timid and shy and backward, eminently unadventurous; so what I still believe must have proved a successful career was never begun.

At home, in the tea trade, there were no careers. There was a certain routine to be followed, but

anybody except a nit-wit could have followed it.
For commerce, I confess, I had little esteem.
Smartness, and the kind of geniality that blos-
soms into dirty stories, seemed the most valuable
assets there; intelligence was a negligible quantity,
and integrity a drawback. Of course, except in the
busy season, my evenings were free; and in these
spare hours, and on Sundays, I read a great deal,
and I wrote.

In *Apostate* I have described my first literary
efforts. They were disappointing, but I continued
in much the same way, and for the same reason—
because I liked writing, and because it brought
other things I cared for closer to me. But I was
far from precocious, everything I learned was
learned slowly, a more tortoise-like progress
could scarcely be imagined. In the small back
room at home which I used as a study, and whose
walls I had covered with posters by Dudley
Hardy, Mucha, and Steinlen (for the poster was
then in its prime)—a room whose only furniture
was a round table (actually our old nursery table),
two chairs, and some shelves I had hammered up
in a recess—slowly, night by night, I produced
The River. Eden Phillpotts has written a novel
called *The River*, but the only person except its
author who ever read *my River* was Andrew
Rutherford, the boy of whom I have spoken,
without naming him, in the last chapter of *Apostate*. Andrew was my great friend. As apprentices
we had been together for nearly two years: then

he had left business to go to Queen's University, and from Queen's he had gone to Edinburgh, leaving me nearly as lonely as before I had met him. It is true there were the vacations, but these he usually spent at the seaside. Moreover, when he *was* at home, he liked to work in the evenings, and the evenings were my only free time. He seemed perfectly content with this arrangement; I was not; and in fact nothing was ever again the same. I could not forget the old days; I could not reconcile myself to the change. He, on the other hand, could not, or would not, admit that there *had* been any change. Nevertheless, slowly but surely, we drifted apart. He had always been primarily intellectual, and as the years passed he grew more and more so. Our friendship continued, but it was now definitely on the so reasonable, so undemonstrative plane where he had chosen to set it. It made no demands (on one side); it accepted quite contentedly long periods of separation; to me it seemed inhuman. I was not made that way; I stumbled and blundered, and could find no happiness in it; and inevitably I was always putting myself in the wrong, taking offence, being hurt, and showing that I was. Acceptance came with time, but one strange—yet perhaps not really strange—result was that the old half-forgotten dream-life, which had been blotted out, began to resume its sway.

I gave Andrew *The River* to read, and with the exception of the first chapter, which was purely descriptive, he disliked it. This did not disappoint me, for I agreed with him: I had never even thought of trying to get it published, and had only lent him the manuscript because he had pressed me to do so. What I needed, however, was not a mere confirmation of my own judgement, but a practical criticism, which would have shown me that I was definitely on the wrong path, and how and why it was wrong. For it was not revision that was required, it was a complete alteration of method, manner, and aim. I was imitating the wrong models, and imitating them very badly. The prose I admired was rich and exotic, the prose of Pater and d'Annunzio. My mind was immature, my taste was immature, and my education insufficient. I tried to reproduce the effects that appealed to me, and in the attempt to achieve poetic beauty employed a vicious medium that was neither poetry nor prose. I had no rhythm of my own, and as I was extremely susceptible to rhythm, followed whatever tune happened to be haunting my mind at the moment. Then, quite by chance, I discovered Henry James, who introduced fresh complications and a new rhythm.

It was in these inauspicious circumstances and with these handicaps that I laboriously produced my next novel, *The Kingdom of Twilight*. The pretentious title points to d'Annunzio, the opening sentence is pure Henry James. I detest this book; I am glad it is forgotten; and when I could do so with safety I have destroyed any copies I could

lay my hands on. But there is no use pretending
that while I was writing it I did not hope and
sometimes believe it was good. What, if any, were
its earlier adventures, I cannot remember. I expect
it went to several publishers. I know I could not
afford to have it typed, and that it was eventually
brought out by Fisher Unwin as vol. IX in his
First Novel Library.

This series had met with some success. It was,
of course, purely a publisher's stunt, and followed
the same firm's Pseudonym and Autonym Libraries, in the former of which will be found at
least one work of distinction—a short novel by
Ganconagh, who was W. B. Yeats. I cannot say
how many first novels were issued in all, but by
the time vol. IX was reached the public, I fancy,
had had more than enough of them. The books
were uniformly bound in pale green boards, with
square spines, a feature of the binding being that
it rapidly detached itself from the contents. I did
not like the "get-up", which struck me as cheap
and flimsy. The format of the Pseudonym and
Autonym Libraries had been rather charming—
a kind of Elzevir—but the First Novel Library
suggested mass production. However, to receive
the proofs of any first book is, I expect, an ex-
citing experience. I certainly was excited, and so
impetuous that I made a mess of them. In the
event, this haste proved completely unnecessary,
for the publication of the novel was postponed.
I wrote a letter of expostulation, but actually—I

know not why—vol. X appeared before vol. IX, and a further period elapsed before I received, as a sop to my impatience, an advance copy of the tale.

Again I need not have been in a hurry. Eagerly I began to read, and I had read very few pages before the blow fell. The typographical blunders, which extended even to the name of one of the characters, were as the sands of the sea; but it was not these, it was the whole book that sickened me. How, in the space of a few months, could I have so completely outgrown it! For I had. It seemed to me a hotch-potch of purple patches, childish gush, and childish sentimentality. The disappointment was sharp—so sharp that I wanted, while there was still time, to have the novel suppressed. But I could not do this unless I bought up the entire edition myself, which obviously was impossible. On the other hand, I did not see how the publishers themselves could want to issue it. As a specimen of book production it would do them no credit, and I supposed such things must matter. I could alter it, and they could bring it out then; or what would be still better, I could give them another book instead. Yet I did not really believe they would consent. I was inexperienced, but not so inexperienced as all that. On the other hand, any effort seemed better than none, so in a mood of deepest depression I wrote to Andrew, enclosing a letter which I asked him to forward if he approved of it.

He didn't, and I might have known he
wouldn't. For after all he had read the manuscript and liked it. He had read it in instalments
while I was writing it: he had read it again when
it was finished, and still he had liked it. Of course,
I too had liked it then, but I couldn't go *on* liking
it, there was a limit. And what, in any case, were
such likings worth? My old nurse Emma, to
whom I sent a copy, liked it, and that, I knew,
must have been sheer self-deception. It contained
nothing that Emma could possibly like, and I had
only sent it to her because I was afraid that if I
didn't, by some chance she might learn of its
existence and feel hurt. I do not mean that Emma
told a lie: I am quite sure she thought she liked it:
but I am equally sure that her favourable judgement was due to a memory of the little boy to
whom she had once told stories, and far better
stories, herself. She lived long enough for me to
send her a copy of *The Garden God*, but not the
book that was really her book, *The Retreat*.

I do not think Andrew's reaction was the same
as Emma's, but certainly it erred in that direction.
He was prejudiced in favour of the author, and
he was naturally kind. Also, though I could never
understand why, though he disliked sentimentality in life, he seemed to be blind to it in literature.
He liked the works of J. M. Barrie; he liked
extremely a once popular and now forgotten
story called *Misunderstood*. I, on the other hand,
who *was* sentimental, found certain passages in

Barrie revolting, though obviously prompted by the tenderest feeling. It was all a matter of expression, of the tact or taste of the artist.

Not that the faults of *The Kingdom of Twilight* were by any means limited to faults of sentiment; they appeared to me to embrace everything—which in a sense cleared the ground. My only consolation was that I saw them, and therefore, I hoped, could never write quite so bad a book again.

Andrew defended it. "I am really angry with you," he wrote. "Your conduct is simply preposterous. You have written an admirable novel—a novel of which you have every right to be proud—and now at the last moment you commence running it down in an extremely foolish and unintelligent manner. It is ridiculous of you to write and tell me that there are only about forty pages of it worth reading (actually this estimate was too high); I have read it myself and I know—a great deal better than you do at present evidently—how good it is. I haven't the slightest doubt that in three or four months you will see that I am right and you are altogether wrong. That your book appears to you as it does at the moment is really your fault, not its. And don't talk any more nonsense about having put my name at the beginning. I am extremely glad that you did. I like the book, if you don't.

"It is unfortunate the mistakes you refer to were not corrected. The printers may be able to do something yet, but if not, no good will be done by your worrying yourself to death about the matter."

This, the verdict of friendship, did not alter my opinion. Nevertheless, it must have had some reconciliatory effect, for a copy of the thing was dispatched to Henry James, and from Lamb House, Rye also I received a kindly note, though the allusion to my handwriting bothered me a good deal. His own, in huge, slanting, nearly indecipherable characters sprawled across the page, with about two words to a line, and I wished I had been a little more careless.

Dear Mr. Forrest Reid,

I am obliged to you for your offering of *The Kingdom of Twilight*, with its accompanying letter (in so beautiful a hand!), and am happily able to tell you that I have—and not otherwise than promptly—read your book, and with interest and attention. The very commendable source of its interest seems to me to be that, up to the middle at least, you see your subject where it *is*—in the character and situation of your young man—that is, in the development and spectacle of these; and that, so seeing it, you stick to it with artistic fidelity and consistency. I confess, however, that *after* the middle, you strike me as *losing* your subject—or, at any rate, I, as your reader, did so. After the meeting with the woman by the sea—certainly after the parting from her—I felt the reality of the thing deviate, felt the subject

lose its conditions, so to speak, its *observed* character and its logic. There are too many things I
don't follow, and, I can't but think, too many
aberrations and perversities of proportion. However, it is not of your young, your airy and
enviably young inexplicitnesses that I wished to
speak—for many of these obviously you will
leave behind you. There are elements of beauty
and sincerity in your volume that remain with me,
and I am very truly yours,

HENRY JAMES.

This pleasant letter certainly cheered me,
though I knew its final words were over-kind.
The sincerity is there, but the beauty is not, while
unfortunately there is a great deal of straining
after beauty, with lamentable results. The criticism
is true in so far as that the book goes all to pieces
once my "young man" reaches the stage of
succumbing to feminine attractions. As in a later
novel, *At the Door of the Gate*, I even plunged him
into the adventures of matrimony and paternity.
In all this I was writing entirely outside my
experience, and even the natural scope of my sympathy, trying to present life as a whole, whereas
I knew only one little corner of it. In fact, sub-
stituting the word "novel" for "poem", what
Doctor Johnson so unwarrantably said of *Lycidas*
seems to me here to apply perfectly—at any rate
to all the latter portion of the tale: "In this poem
there is no nature, for there is no truth; there is no

27

art, for there is nothing new. Its form is that of a pastoral—easy, vulgar, and therefore disgusting."

The direct effect of Henry James's criticism, however, was to encourage me to turn back to my earlier tale, *The River*, in which, so far as the subject went, I had not been working in the dark, not guessing, but treating a situation and a range of emotion that I understood.

In its original form *The River* had been a full-length school story, a forerunner of *Pirates of the Spring*, and why I should have rejected this realistic framework is now hard to see. For though the tale was a failure, that was the fault of the writing, not of the conception. The river itself was the Lagan, which I had known from childhood; the school was my own school; and all the characters that mattered were boys. But when I came to read it over, what happened was that certain passages and scenes stood out like lyrics scattered through a play in prose, and I conceived the idea of detaching these from their realistic setting and presenting them as a kind of reverie. The whole thing had to be rewritten in any case, so why not alter the plan, scrap the naturalistic setting, the minor figures, the school, and work out the central theme in dreamland? I had another reason too. Pater's imaginary portrait, *The Child in the House*, seemed to me then the most lovely thing in all prose literature, and I knew it had been written as the first chapter of a novel of modern life. True, there had never been a second chapter, the novel had been abandoned, but this did not discourage me. I would write *my* novel like that—giving it the unbroken mood and atmosphere of a lyric. After all, d'Annunzio had done this in *The Virgins of the Rocks*, so why should not I? The first thing, then, was to lift the story out of its rather uncouth local surroundings, and place my school somewhere vaguely in England, but not really anywhere, and my holiday scenes equally vaguely in a romantic Ireland, a "kingdom by the sea".

It seems strange to me now that I should have wanted to express myself in the manner of *The Child in the House*, or have thought it possible. For though I must have had that streak in me, on the whole I wasn't a bit that kind of person. I was fairly tough; I was fond of games; I was fond of "ragging". The amusing, not to say the broadly comic side of life appealed strongly to me. Yet no one could possibly gather this from either *The Kingdom of Twilight* or *The Garden God*, which was my new and quite unrecognizable version of *The River*.

The Garden God was an innocent book—conceived and written in a spirit of innocence. I liked it much better than *The Kingdom of Twilight;* I have an idea that I liked it very much indeed; and because of this I wanted to dedicate it to Henry James, who was now the supreme object of my admiration. So I wrote to him, and presently, from America, received his reply.

Butler Place,
Logan Station,
Philadelphia.

Dear Mr. Forrest Reid,

Your note of the 19th May came to me in a far country, and this may very well reach you too late for your book. But I with pleasure assent to the opportunity you offer my good wishes for that volume—****** feeling a visible sign and testimony of them ***** in your possibly being able to carry out your proposal as to the dedication.

Yours very truly,

Henry James.

PS. I return presently to England and should be glad to receive a copy of the book (at Lamb House, Rye).

I consider myself rather a dab at puzzles, and at all events hate to be defeated by them; nevertheless the words I have represented by stars I cannot decipher. It is not for want of trying, nor of appeals to outside aid. I have spent hours pondering on those two missing words (six letters, I think, and five), but I cannot offer even a conjecture as to their identity. The letter, however, did not reach me too late: I wish it had. Not that at this time it much matters. But it did then. Something was lost. I never visited Lamb House, which was a plan that had been mooted and that I abandoned with genuine regret—more than regret. Every printed line the Master had written was in my possession, and I am not referring only to his books. I knew his work inside out. I was probably the only person in the world except himself who did know it like that, or who now ever will. Who else has read *De Grey: a Romance*, *Osborne's Revenge*, *Professor Fargo*, *The Ghostly Rental?* Even *Gabrielle de Bergerac*, a novelette which ran through three numbers of the *Atlantic Monthly*, and really foreshadows the later James, I suspect to be now rather less than a name. These tales, buried in the files of extinct American periodicals, were not easy to acquire, but I acquired them, eighteen of them. *Rejected Stories*, by Henry James, is a good-sized volume, and I imagine only one copy of it exists. The earliest tale, *The Story of a Year*, is dated March 1865. "In early May, two years ago, a young couple I wot of strolled homeward from an evening walk, a long ramble among the peaceful hills which inclosed their rustic home." The manner, you will perceive, is not precisely that of *The Golden Bowl*. Nevertheless, the tale is Henry's.

The fateful letter reached me at a very busy time, when, on a sudden impulse, I had decided to renounce the tea-trade, and was preparing to go to Cambridge. I had no definite plan beyond that. The break was made largely because I felt that I had got into a rut, and that I did not like the rut, and that it would be better to get out of it. My mother's death made this possible. Otherwise my life probably would have taken an entirely different course, and eventually I might have gone to India or Ceylon: more than one chance to do so—connected with tea-planting—having already been put in my way.

III

IT was not until after the publication of my first book that I made friends with anybody who was trying to write, or indeed practise any kind of art. At my prep school—Miss Hardy's—there had been Robert Lynd, but I did not know him well, though I remember walking with him and two other boys to Lisburn and back, along the banks of the Lagan. At my next school, the Royal Academical Institution—always called "Inst"— were J. W. Good and Paul Henry, but the latter, I think, was there only for two or three terms, and at any rate I had merely a nodding acquaintance with both. Lynd and Paul Henry eventually went to London; Good remained at home and joined the staff of a local newspaper, *The Northern Whig*. Those three were friends, but, as I say, I hardly knew them at that time, though later I became friends with Good and Paul Henry—of Lynd I never saw very much.

It was towards the end of my business career that *The Kingdom of Twilight* appeared, and an early result was that I learned of the existence in Belfast of a very minor echo of the Dublin literary and dramatic movement. The Ulster Literary Theatre had been founded, and had produced two plays—*The Reformers*, by David Parkhill, and *Brian of Banba*, by Bulmer Hobson. The experiment was written up in the columns of

The Whig by Good, and in another paper, *The Evening Telegraph*, by Rathcol (W. B. Reynolds). Moreover, in imitation of Yeats's magazine *Samhain*, a literary quarterly called *Ulad* had been started, under the joint editorship of Reynolds and Parkhill, and it was from the former that I received a note asking me to call upon him.

The month was, I think, "the bleak December", and the hour between seven and eight, when I set out to pay this visit. I lived on the Malone Road, Reynolds in lodgings on the Antrim Road, so I had to take two trams and had plenty of opportunity to wonder what he wanted and what he would be like. I was at that time very shy of meeting strangers, but the moment I was shown into his sitting-room I knew there was no cause for alarm. A third person was present, but of him I can remember nothing except that he was sent out at once to the nearest pub to buy a bottle of marsala—then, though not later—the favourite drink of Reynolds—and that throughout the evening he rarely uttered a word.

My first impression of Reynolds was that he looked rather odd. He had thin sandy hair, a smallish face, and large round spectacles through the thick lenses of which he blinked at me benevolently. Years afterwards I described him, under the name of Bingham, in a long short story called *Furnished Apartments*, but I didn't like the story and never published it. Reynolds no doubt was plain, yet to my mind this plainness was completely redeemed by a pleasant and almost childishly innocent expression. He was, in fact, a distinctly pleasant person, and I liked him from the beginning. He told me of the Ulster Renaissance; he told me of the new quarterly that had been started; he gave me a copy of the first number, and he asked me to write something for the second. He had already received poems from A. E. and Padraic Colum; plays from Joseph Campbell, Parkhill, and Bulmer Hobson; he had been promised articles by Stephen Gwynn and Roger Casement; and the Celtic design on the cover was by John Campbell. Reynolds was eloquent, optimistic, and extremely enthusiastic: I felt ignorant, bewildered, and very much out of it. Although Irish, I had never been interested in politics ("a bloody scandal!", as Good used to say later), had never distinguished in my mind north from south, and the Ulster propaganda did not particularly appeal to me. It was not what to-day would be called Ulster propaganda, since it was definitely nationalist, and merely insisted that Ulster should play its part in the Irish Revival. I had no objection to that naturally, but I could not see why there should be two camps, nor why what Reynolds called "the Ulster genius" should necessarily be, as he said it was, satiric. If it came to that, it was the first time I had heard of "the Ulster genius", and I had certainly seen no sign of it. Therefore I listened to Reynolds without conviction. I didn't know what Ulad

meant; I didn't know why Joseph Campbell
should call himself Seosamh MacCathmhaóil. It
seemed to me a most difficult name to pronounce,
and since Reynolds got over that by pronouncing
it Joe, the difficulty still remains. I asked him
what he would like me to write, and received a
sudden clue as to the real bent of his interests
when he replied without a moment's hesitation,
"an essay on *The Future of Irish Opera*."

The suggestion was highly characteristic, but
I did not know this then, and it depressed me.
I didn't believe in either the past, present, or
future of Irish opera. It was not that I couldn't
imagine it; it was rather because I could—in all
its dreadfulness—having once sat through a performance of Stanford's *Shemus O'Brien*. But Irish
opera, like English opera, was a thing to which I
had learned to give a wide berth. Moreover, my
sole qualification for writing about *any* kind of
opera consisted in the fact that I was a devotee,
and made an annual pilgrimage to Covent Garden.
To me this appeared insufficient. Reynolds, however, found it perfectly satisfactory; so I had to
refuse definitely, and imagined the interview to
be at an end. But I did not know my Reynolds.
In the twinkling of an eye opera was dismissed.
The article might deal with any subject I liked, so
long as it related to Ireland—preferably to Ulster,
since the purpose of the magazine was to boost
the Ulster movement.

I must say Reynolds was remarkably good-natured, for my failure to respond continued. It was not due to obstinacy; it was merely that I did not see how writing could ever be anything but the expression of an individuality, while Reynolds, I gathered, thought it should be the expression of the policy and aspirations of a group. He did not share Matthew Arnold's disapproval of thinking in batches of fifty: far from it. Everybody was to write expressing the aims of the group, and from the same point of view—which, in the event, to do him justice, was what actually happened. In the end we compromised, and I agreed to write a paper on the Lane collection of pictures, then on exhibition in the Harcourt Street Gallery in Dublin.

I did so, but I headed it, "Tout paysage est un état d'âme", and I knew it merely shelved the problem, which indeed cropped up again with my contribution to the May number. This was a short story about a little boy, and was called *Pan's Pupil*. I gave it to Reynolds diffidently, and he received it in silence. I guessed what he was thinking while he turned the leaves. There were so many Irish gods, and Pan was not one of them: there were so many little boys who spoke the Ulster dialect, and mine was not one of them. In self-defence I mentioned that I did not talk in dialect myself, and for that matter neither did he, though both of us had been born and had lived all our lives in Ulster. But I could see that to Reynolds the excuse rang hollow. Besides, the

Story was not satiric, and he had this theory about
the Ulster genius firmly embedded in his soul—
had even put it into practice himself by writing
a parody on the overture to *Tannhäuser*, using
Orange tunes as his themes.

Pan's Pupil nevertheless appeared, but my
contributions to the August number did not.
These, though in prose, had been inspired by the
Greek Anthology, and their subjects were grass-
hoppers, trees, dogs, and our old friend the
Lagan. If I couldn't be more Ulster than that!
the expression on the face of Reynolds seemed
to reproach me. And yet they *were* Ulster. The
grasshopper was as busy and as happy on the
banks of the Lagan as ever he had been on those
of the Ilissos, and it wasn't my fault if he still
played the same music. The things had been
written on the spot, with my eye on the object,
and as the spirit moved me. I admit they were
also written with the feeling that if the members
of the *Ulad* council didn't like them they could
do the other thing.

The visit Reynolds paid me to announce that
they *didn't* like them was memorable. From the
hushed solemnity of his manner my first impression was that something tragic must have happened, and that he wanted to break the news very
gently. Parkhill, who was with him, looked on in
a kind of irritated aloofness. But presently he
interrupted the rather elaborate preamble in
which Reynolds was displaying so much tact, and

said bluntly that if I wanted the things to go in they *would* go in, but there had been the hell of a row about them, and there would be another. He and Reynolds were prepared to back me up to the point of wrecking the magazine—and that was all.

Parkhill looked cross; Reynolds, for the only time that I remember, looked curiously religious. Fortunately the situation was eased by the fact that I didn't care whether they appeared or not. Nobody was paid for contributing, so I should lose nothing; I was on the point of going to Cambridge; I was correcting the proofs of *The Garden God*; Henry Newbolt had accepted an essay I had written for *The Monthly Review;* Arthur Symons had gone out of his way to write me a very kind note about it; and Robert Cromie had even reviewed the essay, and at the same time cracked me up generally, in *The Whig*. All this I had found extremely pleasant, and being somewhat mercurial, never doubted but that it would continue. So without ill-feeling on either side I retired from *Ulad*, and heard no more of the magazine until some six months later, at Cambridge, when I received a letter inviting me to edit it. I don't know what had happened in the meantime; evidently an embroilment of some kind; but I was too busy to undertake the proposed task, and *Ulad* expired, having run as long a course as such ventures usually do. It was attractive while it lasted—well-printed and pleas-

ing to the eye. Strange as this may seem, I am
now inclined to think that it perished largely for
lack of copy. *Pan's Pupil* was the only story that
had appeared in it. Reynolds, Good, Parkhill,
Joseph Campbell, Alice Milligan, Rutherford
Mayne, Gerald Macnamarra—all were busy
writing plays; but a magazine cannot be run on
plays alone, and I don't think anybody except
myself was interested in other literary forms. For
that matter, I didn't really belong to the movement at all. I had been dragged into *Ulad* by
Reynolds and Parkhill, but there my participation
ended.

Not, however, my friendship with Reynolds
and Parkhill—Reynolds in particular, for Parkhill later went out to the South Sea Islands and I
never saw him again, though I received an
occasional postcard, and he came back to drive a
motor ambulance in France during the Great
War.

But I feel this chapter belongs to Reynolds, and
I am going to paint him as I knew him. He was an
idealist and an enthusiast. He was also possessed
of a faith that could very nearly move mountains,
if not the Belfast public. Quite early in this Ulster
business—in fact, on the strength of a couple of
very short, very slender and experimental plays—
he had begun to talk about raising a building-
fund, and had procured, I know not whence,
architectural plans for the new theatre, which he
carried round in his pockets and spread out on the

tables of public-houses. Yet even while he was discussing them, I could see that the theatre arising dream-like in his imagination was an opera house, and that secretly he was listening to an invisible orchestra, and not watching a farm-kitchen comedy. Presently he would be describing a performance of *Tristan*, with Félix Mottl conducting, and Jean de Reszké and Nordica in the chief parts. And sometimes, in more sceptical moments, I wondered if this too were a dream. For really—! Well, Jean de Reszké was before my time, and when and how had this so early visit of Reynolds to London taken place? He was about the same age as I was, certainly no older, and Ternina and Van Dyck were the fixed Wagnerian stars in my boyhood. The amazing thing, however, is that Reynolds himself had an ambition to appear on the stage. Not, I hasten to add, in opera, but in Good's electioneering play, *Leaders of the People*. I don't know that he mentioned this desire to anybody except myself, but he mentioned it to me frequently, and the argument by which it was supported was unusual. He was blind as a bat without his spectacles, would be unable to see even the people in the front row of the stalls, and therefore could not possibly be nervous. And he thought the part of the poet would exactly suit him—a part actually played by T. W., now Judge, Brown.

This ambition, I confess, surprised me, for I felt that the stage presence of Reynolds would be

scarcely more impressive than my own; and
nothing could have induced *me* to risk such an
adventure. On the other hand I knew it was not
prompted by vanity (there was not a spark of
vanity in his nature), but by an enviable and complete absence of self-consciousness, a streak of
childishness, which I, personally, found most
endearing. Once you had grasped it, this was the
key that unlocked every door. And unless you did
grasp it you never really knew him. That is why
most people, and Good in particular, underrated
him. Good rarely mentioned him without a
cynical little chuckle; and it was he, I fancy, who
invented the nickname, Sunny Jim, derived from
a figure in an absurd poster then very much to the
fore, advertising the virtues of some patent tonic
or food. It was certainly apt. "High o'er the fence
leaps Sunny Jim"—and there, undoubtedly, once
the suggestion had been made, was Reynolds
beaming at you from hoardings or the backs of
magazines, radiantly expressive of the joy of life.
But Good did not take him seriously, regarded
him with a kind of tolerant amusement, thought
him lazy; and it is true that he was not ambitious
so far as his newspaper work went. This was
because journalism with Reynolds was a secondary consideration; he knew he had no gift for
writing; he wanted time for his music, and preferred a minor job which gave him this time. He
had neither Good's intellect nor education, but
in his own way he was an artist, and Good, though

42

a brilliant all-round journalist, and a still more brilliant talker, was not. The conversation of Reynolds was less anecdotal, more tentative, and he sometimes said things people are supposed not to say, even when they think them. He once told me, for instance, that he was attractive to women, and though, coming from anybody else, this would have jarred horribly, coming from him I merely found it interesting. "Why, Willie?" I asked. "Why do you attract them?" But after some thought he failed to find a reason. I mentioned that *I* didn't attract them, and he was kind enough to affect an air of slight surprise. I told him that I attracted dogs, which, though it may have sounded humble, was perfectly true. Nor did it excite derision: our friendship, I imagine, was very much that of two preparatory schoolboys: it was simple and it was genuine.

Even in print Reynolds sometimes came out with naïvely Reynoldsonian things. He had written of "the minor poets who infest Dublin", a descriptive phrase which did not endear him to the minor poets: in a dramatic criticism of *A Midsummer Night's Dream* he had said that "Mr. Weir's Bottom was irresistible", a remark which for many a day proved equally irresistible to the vulgar-minded. Nor could he understand my objection to his writing of Mrs. Patrick Campbell as Patrick Campbell. He maintained that it implied a compliment, placed her on the same level as Duse and Sara. There was no use arguing the point. The objection was dismissed as one of those narrow prejudices due simply to my hopelessly conventional upbringing.

Reynolds was not town-bred, and had never had much schooling of any kind. He never talked of the past, but over a period of years I gradually gathered that his father had been a small farmer, and that Willie himself, at the age of fourteen, had been brought to Belfast, where a job had been found for him in one of the big drapers' shops. His subsequent career had been entirely of his own making. When I got to know him he was a musical critic, and writing music of his own. We had first met on the ground of literature, but never afterwards, for, as he admitted himself, he had not really the faintest literary sense. My novels were the only books he ever reviewed, except books on music. Of *Following Darkness* he wrote that it possessed all the finest qualities of the work of the Brontës, Thomas Hardy, Joseph Conrad, Henry James, and Jane Austen. Could anybody ask more? Indeed, to me it suggested even an *embarras de richesse*, and this was not one of the reviews I left lying about. Anatole France says somewhere that Victor Cousin discovered sublimities in Pascal which have since been found to be printer's errors, and Reynolds was like that. He could see whatever he wanted to see, and all his geese were swans. The title, *Following Darkness*, he explained, had been borrowed from "Holy Writ", and like most really good titles had

44

nothing at all to do with the story. Both statements puzzled me. "Holy Writ," of course, I understood. Nothing could have induced Reynolds—pen in hand—to have referred to the Bible simply as the Bible. "Holy Writ" was style. But why had the title nothing to do with the story?

I found him excellent company—easy, unexacting, and natural. Corporeally he was rather sluggish, but spiritually he was alert, adventurous, while the extreme artlessness of his countenance added an element of piquancy and unexpectedness to the more daring flights of his conversation. He preferred to talk in a pub. Not that he drank much, but in a pub he felt at home, like a snail in his shell. He had of course views on the subject, for he had views on all subjects. He liked the murky atmosphere, the smoke-darkened ceiling and woodwork, the complete absence of everything genteel. Music, religion, life—all his favourite topics could be discussed more satisfactorily in a pub. Pubs reminded him of Rembrandt, and of the beauty that could be extracted from the unbeautiful. It was in a pub that he persuaded me to write the libretto of an opera for him, and I wrote it, and he composed the overture, and the music for the first scene, which was in pantomime. This music was played twice at orchestral concerts in the Ulster Hall, with my pantomime directions printed in the programme. Then unfortunately Reynolds went straight on to

45

the love duet, and, having written this, his interest
in the work collapsed.

He now wanted a new libretto, and in the bar
of the Arts Club he gave me an outline of the kind
of thing. It was to be staged amid the snows of
Labrador, and the love duet in the second act was
to take place in a wooden shanty, with ravening
wolves and a frozen world outside. He sketched a
plot, and all I had to do was to write the words—
mere child's play to one so gifted. I objected that
the plot was crude and melodramatic. He admitted that it was both, but that it was what he
wanted. The fault of my first libretto—extracted
from *The Song of Solomon*—was that it hadn't been
vulgar enough. *Tosca*, *Madame Butterfly*, *Aïda*,
Siegfried—they were all vulgar; and the love duet
itself, to be any good, must be a big vulgar tune
such as people would sing in their baths. What
was wrong with me was that I was a snob. He
waited a moment or two before adding, "a spiritual
snob". This definition pleased him. He chuckled
over it to himself, and then, seeing that I too was
impressed, told me that it was a subtlety.

For Reynolds, though some people denied it,
had a sense of humour. It was queer, freakish, and
his jokes came out unexpectedly, accompanied by
a weird little cackle of laughter about as merry-
sounding as churchyard bells. But I liked the
jokes and the laughter, as I liked everything about
him. His humour was individual, boyish, and
devoid of malice or irony. I never in my life heard

him say an ill-natured thing, even when there was plenty of provocation. I waited for him now to develop the theme of spiritual snobbishness. I wasn't quite sure what it meant, but it sounded promising, and anyhow, an analysis of one's own idiosyncrasies, even when unfavourable, is always interesting. But Reynolds blinked at me through his spectacles: I was trying to lure him from the important to the trivial. "*Will* you do the Labrador libretto?" he asked.

"But if it's only to be vulgar," I responded feebly, "why can't you do it yourself?"

This was not intended as a sarcasm, nor was it taken as such. We were alone in the bar, and Reynolds spat dreamily into the gas stove, which fizzled. It was an unconscious trick he had when music was running in his head. From past experience I knew what was coming, and sure enough it came, in a rather cracked and hoarse "Rum-tumty-tum. Rum-tumty-tumty". It was my fault if there were to be no better words, for it was an adumbration of the Labrador love duet. "That's fine," Reynolds said simply on its conclusion.

Now, though in ordinary speech it was far from unpleasant, when raised in song the voice of Reynolds resembled nothing so much as the last water escaping from a bath, therefore I knew he had not done the love duet justice, and that I should have to wait before expressing an opinion. "What about it?" he asked again.

"No," I replied. "I wrote the first libretto

47

because I was interested in it quite apart from the music. My idea was that the music should be more an accompaniment to the words than anything else. Anyhow it's a quite good libretto, and you still have it."

So, I may add, have I; and I can say frankly that I continue to like it, because, beyond the stage directions, it contains not one word of my own composition: all is taken, though with rearrangements and transpositions, from "Holy Writ". But from the beginning it had no luck. Reynolds turned it down: Howard Ferguson, years afterwards, considered it and turned it down: a budding dramatist, who had asked to see it, wished to incorporate it in a play he was writing, and when I refused was highly indignant: it actually was accepted as a play by the B.B.C., but Tyrone Guthrie, who was to have produced it, left the B.B.C., and the arrangement fell through. Now it reposes in peace amongst other discarded efforts—"A cœur blessé—l'ombre et le silence".

To these memories and conversations I'm afraid I can attach no such reliable dates as I can to my impressions of childhood and boyhood. I do my best, but, odd though it may seem, I am not even sure of the year in which Reynolds discovered the secret of perpetual motion. I can remember, however, receiving the news—at the door of the *Telegraph* office in Royal Avenue. It held me spellbound, so that, since it was the busy lunch hour and the door was one of those swing doors, for a minute or two nobody could get either in or out. Finally we were pushed into the street, but I still clung to the inventor, who was going home, and invited me to accompany him. When we were safe on the tram my surprise and congratulations took on a more inquisitive note. For scientific investigation was about the last thing one would have expected from Reynolds.

"Don't you have to be frightfully well up in mathematics and mechanics and physics and all that?" I questioned.

"No," said Reynolds simply; but presently added: "Anyway, I got one or two books from the library."

Yet, as we neared our destination, I saw that he had begun to fidget a little. "Of course, it doesn't quite work yet. I mean—not perfectly."

I was undiscouraged, and assured him that I hadn't supposed it did.

This I said in all innocence, but he looked at me suspiciously. Spectacles can be extraordinarily expressive.

"What do you mean by you hadn't supposed it did?"

"Well, I hadn't."

"Hadn't what?"

"Supposed it did."

He grunted, but did not press me further, and he distinctly brightened up again when we reached the house. He had been married for some years now: indeed one of his boys was called after me.

But it was to the offspring of his genius he wished to introduce me on that afternoon, and for this purpose took me to the room upstairs where he worked.

The thing really was beautifully made—of white wood—and Reynolds had made it himself. It resembled a miniature circular switch-back, and to demonstrate the discovery there were coloured glass marbles, one of which he now set in motion. It is true that the motion was not exactly perpetual, but it did go on for quite a long time—something approaching a minute I should think—and it was so far perpetual that as soon as it stopped Reynolds immediately started it again. It was most ingenious, and I admired it sincerely. Unfortunately I said the wrong thing: I asked if the children had seen it.

Reynolds, who had been quite happy, took this as an innuendo. "I may tell you that it very nearly worked," he said. "There *is* such a thing as perpetual motion. Otherwise the whole universe would come to a standstill."

"But how do you know it won't?" I asked. "Isn't it generally supposed that it will?"

"It hasn't so far," he replied.

"No, but—— However, of course I know nothing about it; and at any rate it doesn't apply to your machine. What you're after is a motion that continues without any sign of running down."

"You don't think it worth going on with?"

"Well—— You see—— Even compared with an eight-day clock——"

I knew, whether he wanted me to say it or not, it was what he thought himself. "Your music——" I began.

"What's the use of going on with that either?" he interrupted. "It never comes to anything. What's the use of writing music that is never published and never played? I've had one song published, and I've been working for years. I've had a few things played at concerts from manuscript scores, and that's all."

It was the only time I ever heard him making a complaint.

IV

MY main idea about the Cambridge scheme was that it would give me a breathing space during which, for the first two years at least, I need not worry about the future. Andrew was more definite; it was he who now mapped out my whole course and decided that I was going to be a schoolmaster. This decision I accepted, even though secretly I had no faith in it. Somehow I could not picture myself as a schoolmaster, except perhaps in a village-school near the sea, with pupils like little Jude Fawley. But when I mentioned the village-school it was turned down on social grounds: I should be cutting myself off from my own class. For Andrew was getting increasingly worldly and less and less inclined to trust in providence. For the rest, he was in his element, consulting University Calendars, weighing the merits of different triposes, picking out a college. The Modern and Medieval Languages Tripos seemed to him the most suitable for me, and the college he eventually found was Christ's. Actually, neither of us knew anything about any of the colleges, and though doubtless I noted the fact that Milton had been at Christ's, this was most unlikely to have influenced Andrew. But I accepted his judgement with a docility that smacked of fatalism.

The chief, and indeed the only difficulty was to

acquire during the next month or two enough
algebra to pass the Littlego. This Andrew under-
took to drum into me himself—no light task, for at
school I had given up algebra as hopeless, and had
long since forgotten the few rudiments I had ever
known. Once the Littlego was over, however, I
should be able to drop mathematics, and, by some
godsend, Paley's *Evidences of Christianity* figured on
the same paper. Yet even with Paley to help me out
we both felt uneasy. I managed to scrape through,
nevertheless, so all was well.

One of the first steps in my University career
was to seek an interview with Roberts of the
Appointments Board, and that again, I should
think, must have been due to Andrew. Roberts
was genial and cheery, with an air of being
tremendously business-like and practical that
somehow didn't impress me. (It is to be remembered that I was from the north of Ireland.) He
told me to be as imitative as possible, and to pick
up all the little tricks of speech and manner I
could. This counsel may have been wise, but it
struck me as infinitely dismal, and at any rate it
was the last I was likely to follow. I wondered
whether he told everybody this, or whether I had
been singled out because of glaring rusticities. I
had a premonition that nothing very dazzling
would ever come my way through the Appointments Board; and this at least proved correct,
though I had a second interview after taking my
degree. For a few months I received an occasional

notice of a vacant scholastic post in Shanghai or
some such spot, but if I had decided against tea-
planting in Ceylon, it wasn't that I might take up
schoolmastering in Shanghai.

It is perhaps strange that this Cambridge interlude produced upon me so little effect either
outwardly or within, though I suppose it was
partly because I went there too late and took my
own world with me. I enjoyed myself well enough,
but not nearly so well as I had at school. Theo
Bartholomew was the only intimate friend I made,
and the only friend with whom I continued to
keep in touch after I came down. Christ's, too,
turned out to be the wrong college after all—for
me at any rate—and I have never visited it since.

It is hard to tell, of course, but I cannot help
thinking that my years at Cambridge must have
coincided with a particularly unliterary period.
Indeed, one of the things that most struck me was
the almost total absence of any genuine interest in
literature, either early or contemporary. It was an
object of study, but for neither dons nor under-
graduates was it a living thing. I am talking of
English and French literature: on the classical
side there was probably more sensitiveness. As
for actual writing—well, at King's there was
Osbert Burdett, who was working on an extremely bad novel, which I read, finding only one good
sentence in it. (I conscientiously pointed out this
sentence to the author.) To King's also, in my
last year, came Rupert Brooke, and to Trinity

Hall, Ronald Firbank. But upon these swallows alone depended whatever summer there might be, and they were as yet far from fully-fledged. Somehow I didn't believe they ever would be swallows that mattered much; in fact I doubted if Firbank were a swallow at all. Brooke I thought would achieve something; Burdett I thought would become the Burdett he actually became; but Firbank left me in the dark. He was so bad that he might easily become much better than either of the other two, for he had the conscience and determination of an artist: on the other hand, he might still more easily fizzle out. Yet it was of him I saw most, though nobody, I should think, can ever have been less of my kind. I liked him up to a point. That is to say, he never bored me, on the contrary he interested me—but he struck me as extraordinarily feline and sophisticated. Lord Alfred Douglas had given him two or three books to review for a paper called, I think, *The Academy*; and I can remember his fitful and half-comical struggles with a volume on Memlinc. He wanted to condemn the book, which he felt instinctively to be a bad book, yet he did not know enough about the subject to do so with safety. His short stories were produced with equal difficulty, and their psychology, or rather the psychology of their author, I could not fathom, nor can I, I confess, fathom it to-day. Firbank seemed to me unreal. I had never before met anybody in the least like him, and the polished surface was not merely protective but extremely baffling. The only time I ever saw the mask drop was on one winter evening, when, coming out of my sitting-room into the dimly-lit hall, he barked his shins on a coal-scuttle left there by my landlady. Then he said "damn" quite savagely and naturally—as he might have at the age of fourteen—but a moment later the mask was resumed.

I expect he really thought me half-civilized. The first time I dined with him in his rooms at Trinity Hall the table was strewn with orchids and he himself was in evening dress. I unfortunately was not (after all I knew there were to be only the two of us), so he hastily donned a blazer, for at least he had excellent manners. Nevertheless, I felt that I had been guilty of a solecism and was annoyed. I said I had come straight on from a lecture, which alas! was not true, and moreover not even conceivable. But Firbank never expected the truth. "The worst of this place," he replied charmingly, "is that sometimes people dress and sometimes they don't, so one never knows what to do." I hastened to agree with him, and the matter was dismissed.

The dinner was elaborate—with a waiter—or he may have been a gyp; in which case he was a gyp of superior variety—in attendance. On its conclusion Firbank sat on the hearthrug and smoked "drugged cigarettes"; I sat in an arm-chair and smoked a pipe. To me it was a strange evening, and I shouldn't have been surprised if

Dorian Gray had dropped in. Somebody called Brocklehurst, as a matter of fact, did drop in for a minute or two, but I was not introduced to him—an omission Firbank explained later, on the grounds that it seemed silly to introduce people when it was only a matter of saying "How do you do?" The excuse was quite reasonable, yet I suspected its veracity.

Firbank had been staying in Paris with M. de Max, the actor. He had met, or at any rate seen, various celebrities. He talked of Catulle Mendès and Pierre Louÿs. Occasionally there was a sentence in French, which he spoke beautifully. He read me a story he had written about a woman who decides to go into a convent, and then, for an equally frivolous reason, decides to come out again. He was gay, restless, elaborate. And suddenly, beneath it all, I divined that he was intensely nervous. But why? I could not make it out. Why on earth should he be nervous with *me*? Nevertheless he was.

I don't know what sort of time Firbank had at Cambridge. He was a member of the Pitt, which was extremely exclusive. Members of the Pitt were difficult to get to know, and Firbank, as I have hinted, evidently had decided not to introduce me to his other friends. Once, at least, his rooms were ragged, and once, on a foggy November evening, I saw him in the grip of an intoxicated undergraduate, who was shaking him slowly backwards and forwards beneath a lamp in

Trinity Street, and at the same time summing up a view of his character in realistic and unprintable terms. I myself find him difficult to sum up. He had the air of being witty without really being witty. It was the manner more than anything else; his good things would not bear repetition, and his range was extremely limited. Yet he must have been genuine after his fashion, for he never deviated from his course, his later books show only a development of what had been there from the beginning. E. M. Forster, in *Abinger Harvest*, says he had genius, but he hadn't—not a glimmer of it. He was fastidious, and he had a streak of talent, but he never wrote anything that had not before been better done by somebody else. He was a decadent of the school of Oscar Wilde, but lacking Wilde's intellect. I see him hovering between Wilde and Norman Douglas. There is nothing in his books that is not in *The Importance of Being Earnest* and *South Wind*.

Cambridge, I cannot deny, disappointed me. I joined the Irish Society, and attended two or three meetings. I even read a paper on Yeats—a name unknown to the Irish Society—and afterwards read *The Land of Heart's Desire*. There followed the usual discussion, but the only point discussed was whether the fairy child had broken the laws of hospitality or not. I never went back, and am glad to say never paid my subscription.

Then I sampled another society, a feeble thing called The Mermaid, ostensibly literary, but actually utilitarian, the idea being to read plays and poems, not with a view to enjoyment, but because one was taking a literary tripos. At the meetings of The Mermaid occasionally Skeat or some other don would put in an appearance to provide encouragement, and a discussion might then ensue on poetic drama. Indeed, I remember asking Skeat his opinion on two poetic dramas, *The Countess Cathleen*, by Yeats, and *The Return of Ulysses*, by Robert Bridges. Immediately afterwards I regretted having done so. He looked very worried, had heard of neither, and murmured something about Sheridan Knowles being perhaps the best of the moderns.

This, I am afraid, was characteristic. Literature belonged to the past; and its exponents approached it as one might the stuffed birds and beasts in a museum. Yet Skeat himself was very much alive. As a lecturer nobody went to hear him, because his subject, Anglo-Saxon, was so dull; and anyhow could be made up more comfortably in an armchair from text-books. I have been in his class when there were present only myself and one other, yet gallantly he gave his lecture. What really moved my admiration was his prodigious memory. I had in those days a fairly good memory myself, but to watch Skeat tracing the origin of some word, and covering the blackboard with specimens from every language that has ever been spoken, was like watching a conjuring trick. And all the time he would chuckle to himself, taking a quite understandable pleasure in his own dexterity. In appearance he reminded me a little of Blake's drawing of the Ancient of Days, though there was something boyish, something innocent about him, and his blue eyes were bright as a child's. A man who passes his whole life exclusively preoccupied with intellectual studies, does, perhaps, retain this air of innocency. But Skeat also had an amazing vitality; he walked eagerly, quickly, never recognizing anybody he met, his head bent forward, his long white beard floating in the wind. On one evening in each week he was at home to any student who might care to call upon him; and I fancy not many did call, for I distinctly remember that the reception I received was enthusiastic. He liked to show his treasures, his editions of Chaucer. I had come with a number of difficulties encountered in some early Scotch poems, and it was as if I had brought a bone to a dog. He seized on the difficulties, he worried them, he rent them to shreds, and looked delightfully happy. He ran to his bookshelves, climbed on to an arm-chair, and stood lightly poised with one foot on its back while he reached down a volume from a row near the ceiling. The first time I witnessed this feat I felt distinctly alarmed, but he leaped to the ground with the ease of a professional gymnast, and later I grew accustomed to it.

It was from Skeat that I got the suggestion for Professor Heron in *Pender*. I wanted somebody who might make the boy Trefusis possible. For

Trefusis is an anachronism, being founded on the once celebrated Master Romney Robinson, and his poems are imitated from Romney's actual poems. Skeat, as parent, seemed to make him not only possible but inevitable.

The Mermaid I abandoned as I had abandoned the Irish Society. Cambridge was failing me rather badly—on the modern side at all events. One curious thing I discovered was that nobody could read poetry aloud, even though professing to delight in it. I was accustomed to the Irish method—to that of Yeats and Colum—which does full justice to, and sometimes even improvises on, the tune. The English method was to ignore the tune completely. I remember an afternoon at Magdalene when I listened to A. C. Benson reading lyric after lyric in his clear, cultured voice, and as he did so robbing each of its music, till I longed to snatch the book out of his hands. I remember a morning when, in the middle of Donegall Place, Colum chanted in my ear a ballade of Andrew Lang's:

> Oh, where are the endless Romances
> Our grandmothers used to adore?
> The Knights with their helms and their lances,
> Their shields and the favours they wore?
> And the Monks with their magical lore?
> They have passed to Oblivion and *Nox*,
> They have fled to the shadowy shore,——
> They are all in the Fourpenny Box!

and how it had a caressing beauty of sound such as Pachmann used to draw from a piano.

Colum was the best speaker of verse I have ever heard. Yeats was better in his own poems, because his voice could convey the full richness of an orchestra, but Colum could turn the lightest verse to music. A. E.'s method I never admired: he chanted everything in the same solemn monotone, whether it were *Three Blind Mice* or the opening sentence of Saint John's Gospel.

Of the lectures I attended at Cambridge, those of Israel Gollancz were by far the most popular. They were lively and punctuated with jokes, and the classroom was always crowded. They were indeed admirable of their kind, for Gollancz knew his subject, and by enthusiasm sought to create enthusiasm. Unfortunately, their kind was not mine. The Middle English poem he was expounding was better than the idiotic Old French poem which was the subject of Braunholtz's lectures, but would anybody except a student of philology read either for pleasure? So I preferred Braunholtz, who at least did not pretend to find an aesthetic value in the absurd adventures of the absurd Méraugis. Gollancz, on the other hand, expatiating on his Middle English poem, did. A blade of grass had only to be mentioned and we had a rhapsody on a marvellous feeling for nature, which obviously wasn't there. It was not until the appointment of G. C. Macaulay (father of Miss Rose Macaulay, the distinguished novelist), a year before I went down, that I actually enjoyed attending lectures, and found somebody to whom I could listen in an atmosphere that breathed nothing of examinations either past or to come. There are people with whom one feels an instantaneous sympathy. I don't know what this feeling is based on, but I know it has never betrayed me yet. It is something intuitive and profound—a kind of recognition. At all events, I became immediately the follower and supporter of Macaulay, nor was I surprised to find that I had the field very much to myself. At the same time I was annoyed, and particularly so when I heard his lectures condemned on all sides as dull. They were not dull. They were quiet, but there was always the charm of his voice and manner—with something more—a kind of grave distinction. He lectured on Shakespeare, and I knew that he expressed what he felt. I can't remember whether I took many notes: probably not: but if I didn't, it wasn't because I was inattentive. He was talking about a great poet—talking sensitively and with understanding. He was aloof, a little remote, and yet, through this, I divined something intimate, something that I found infinitely preferable to the oriental ebullience of Gollancz. Once he took me with him to the University Library to look up some metrical point concerning Shakespeare's later verse. His manner on that occasion was subtly altered, not in the least distant, but only charming. He lived, I think, a little way out of Cambridge town, and I very much wanted him to ask me to go to see him. He didn't, however, and

I was far too shy to suggest it myself. Yet I found him very kind, not only then but after I had gone down, and I am sure I might have made the suggestion with safety. Only there were so many unwritten rules and conventions, so many things one was supposed not to do, and I had an idea (probably perfectly correct) that this might easily be one of them. I have forgotten what I wanted to talk to him about, but almost certainly it was about writing; and I knew there was no chance unless I paid him a special visit.

I might have given him my new book—*The Garden God*—had I not by this time ceased to give it to anybody. It had appeared in my first or second term, and I had given it to Gollancz, for no better reason than because he had met me in the Union while I was clasping a copy to my breast, and had expressed a curiosity to know what it was. And there and then he had got me to sign it for his special collection of presentation works, little knowing what he was asking for. I didn't know either, for though I had written the thing, it had never dawned upon me that it might possibly offend. At our next meeting his manner was peculiar—slightly constrained, slightly ironical, slightly chilly—and he said not a word about the book. So, rather drearily, I guessed that he must have read it; for in the meantime I had heard from the Master at Lamb House, Rye.

V

AND the Master was not pleased.

The only kind word he had to say was that the book was gracefully written, and it seemed a marvel that he should have brought himself to say even this, for it was clear that it had produced in him an intense exasperation—all the greater because he would not come out into the open and let me have the cause of his annoyance plump and plain.

Strange that this slender tale, removed from actuality and placed in an eternal summer, should have been regarded as a dangerous and subversive work. Whom could it possibly harm? Even to-day I cannot tell you, nor conjecture why it should have been condemned when, fourteen years earlier, Howard Sturgis's *Tim* had been one of the most successful novels of its year. For the two books, spiritually and morally, are on the same plane. Henry James, indeed, contrived to see both the dangerousness and the innocence, thus establishing two grounds for complaint. With what might almost be accounted perversity, it was the latter quality that he censured directly. For obviously the real source of worry was the subject, not the fact that I had left it somewhere in the clouds.

I had left it there because that was where I saw it—half dream, half reality—not because I had any doubts or timidities. It must be remembered that I had been born and bred in an unsophisticated land, that I had received none of the advantages of an English public school education. I wrote the story completely without misgiving, unconscious even that there was anything unusual in the emotion it described. This had been familiar to me from my earliest days, and though it seemed to be generally ignored, I had found it expressed in the Platonic philosophy. Why, then, should what had been academically acceptable for over two thousand years suddenly cease to be acceptable because I had translated it out of the world of dialectic into that of fiction? I had not altered it. It had been formulated by Socrates as an ideal, and as an ideal I had kept it. "It is through love that all the converse of God with man, whether awake or asleep, is carried on. The wisdom which understands this is spiritual. . . . For you may say generally that all desire of good and happiness is only the great and subtle power of love." It is while gazing on his beloved that the eyes of the lover are opened "to see the true beauty—the divine beauty, pure and clear and unalloyed".

Doubtless my own idea was not quite Plato's, because it was in the love itself that I found the divine beauty and goodness. I did not think of it as a stepping-stone to higher things, for the simple reason that I could not conceive of anything higher. All it could gain by being trans-

66

ferred to a timeless, changeless world was the quality of permanence: otherwise it would remain the same. Therefore, why was Plato not condemned? (I had not at that time read Macaulay's essay in which he *is* condemned, straightforwardly if smugly.) On the contrary, the peculiar beauty of the Platonic conception of love was extolled and accepted as an aspect of the Greek genius. And to me it even seemed an aspect that explained much of the difference between Greek art and modern art—certainly the choice of subject. I clung to my conviction, distressed but unshaken.

Yet Henry James's attitude depressed me. It was as if I had bitterly disappointed him, and after all I was his disciple. At that time my enthusiasm for his writings was unbounded. I knew they were not popular, for he had told me so himself in the first letter I ever received from him, but this had only endeared them to me still more. I was like Coleridge, of whom Hazlitt grumbled that he "somehow always contrived to prefer the *unknown* to the *known*". It was not merely an admiration for the artist that I felt: mingled with this was a much more personal feeling—a sympathy with the moral and spiritual qualities that were the standards by which all his characters were judged. The beauty of *The Spoils of Poynton* was not only a beauty of writing and treatment, but also a moral beauty that found expression in the loyalty and intelligence of Fleda Vetch. I, too,

wished to express that moral beauty, therefore it
had been with something like suspense that I had
awaited the verdict from Lamb House. That verdict was what really mattered, and now to find I
had failed, not only in the expression, but in the
very nature of my conception of moral beauty,
left me at a loss, like a small boy who has been
punished for a fault of whose character he is only
dimly aware.

To the general reception of the book I was, in
comparison, indifferent. Also, amid the fuss and
difficulty of working for the Littlego, storing my
belongings and transferring myself to Cambridge,
I had been extraordinarily slack about business
details. Encouraged by David Nutt's pleasant
letter accepting the book, I had left everything to
him. The arrangement was to be on the half-
profit basis, but I never received a signed agreement, though later I wrote frequently asking for
one. And in the matter of accounts it was the
same. The book was published at fifteen shillings,
which seemed to me an absurd price for a story
of about thirty thousand words, and from first to
to last I was paid nothing. I got twelve free copies
on the day of publication and there the matter
ended.

So much for the commercial side, but that was
still an affair of the future; what I had to face
immediately was the consternation I appeared
to have created at Lamb House. I pored over the
fateful letter. This, indeed, was necessary, because

its writer seemed either unable or unwilling to say
clearly what was wrong. I recalled earlier communications which had opened with the friendly
greeting, "My dear young man"; but from the
first words of this, it was plain that I was no
longer anybody's dear young man. Far from it!
Troubled, astonished, disillusioned, I read the
involved sentences again and again. On the surface they were merely chilly, but beneath the
surface it was not hard to divine an intense irrita-
tion. The direct, the open criticism was that the
book should not have followed *The Kingdom of
Twilight*. It seemed to have been written before it,
and, if not, then I had lost ground instead of
gaining it. Nor had I even treated my subject—
such as it was: my characters were not boys, they
were children, and the whole thing was too slight
and immature to be taken for a moment seriously.

Now this would have been all very well if it
hadn't been taken seriously. But only too obviously it had, and the repressed exasperation produced a painful effect upon me, though for a
reason that had nothing whatever to do with
wounded literary vanity. What I felt was that
something had been destroyed—something much
more closely connected with my feeling for the
writer than with my own ambitions. I should
never again be able to regard Henry James in
quite the same way; my admiration for the artist
remained, but an admiration more human and
intimate had been lost. The intelligence that had

seemed so understanding seemed now less understanding. Or perhaps I should say less courageous,
less sympathetic; more worldly, more conventional. Yet I knew that if there had been no
dedication the tone of the letter would have been
different. The dedication, I suppose, had created
a "disconcerting" situation. Years afterwards,
André Raffalovich wrote to me: "He must have
treated you to one of his panics. He once called
on the Beardsleys, and Aubrey's sister (a beautiful
and charming girl) pointed out to him on the
stairs a Japanese print which shocked him. He
called it a 'disconcerting incident' and always
afterwards fought shy of her, though the print
on the stairs was nothing startling. I remember
once teasing him with a friend to know what the
Olympian young man in *In the Cage* had done
wrong. He swore he did not know, he would
rather not know."

In the preface to *The Turn of the Screw* he makes
indeed the same protest of ignorance, which cannot be sincere, since the internal evidence of the
story points to a quite definite knowledge. The
attitude appears to be prompted by a strange
moral timidity, which refuses to accept responsibility for what deliberately has been suggested.

The reaction to my unfortunate dedication was,
I fancy, due to this cause. To have said so bluntly,
however, would to Henry James have been
temperamentally impossible. So he complained
that I hadn't treated my subject. And certainly I

hadn't as he *saw* my subject. But I had treated it as *I* had seen it; I had shirked nothing. If my hero was childish that was due to his environment, his upbringing; or perhaps I should say to mine. Besides, as he must have known, I wasn't trying to write a realistic novel: the purpose of the book was purely lyrical.

Moreover, the knowledge that I had written something that it would have been wiser to have left unwritten was brought home to me through various other channels from day to day. In its frankest and most friendly form it reached me in a letter from Edmund Gosse. Gosse's letter was very different in tone from Henry James's. True, the book had not been dedicated to him, but I believe it would have been different in any case.

> 17 *Hanover Terrace,*
> *Regent's Park.*

Dear Sir,

My only chance of finding time to read the book you have been so kind as to send me was to read it at once: and I had no inclination to drop it when I had taken it up. I found it carefully and delicately written, with an attention to form of which ninety-nine out of every hundred persons who write in these days are as incapable as they are indifferent. I thought that you avoided very cleverly, by occasional points of colloquialism and homely touches, the over-waxen sweetness and smoothness that are the danger of this sort of writing. I thought that it (the little book) was a thing skilfully accomplished, and (if you are young) marvellously promising.

But the mere technique of a book is not everything, and of course the substance, the temper of your dream-extravaganza is much. I dare say that to you it is everything. I cannot find words, easily and blindly, to discuss such a substance or enter into such a temper. I believe I trace beneath your sentences a great deal of doubt, of isolation, perhaps of sorrow and pain. I give my respect and sympathy to that. Everybody must work out his own salvation—he must not let it be damnation. But I am a grey-headed old individualist; I believe in liberty, in the real archaic liberty of every man to be a law unto himself. Yet there must be no interference—that is the essence of liberty—with the rights of others. And for people too obstinately *themselves*, there is always Dreamland, where no one can be hurt, and all things are innocent.

I venture to hope for your happiness, and, if you are ambitious, literary success.

Pray believe me to be
Yours very faithfully
EDMUND GOSSE.

This letter, for which I still feel grateful, helped me in a way that perhaps the writer of it may not have foreseen, though I dimly suspect that he did. He may even—and very easily—have known

how the book had been welcomed in another
quarter, from which I had hoped so much more
and received so much less. Yet years and years
later, after the publication of *Apostate*, Gosse told
me that Henry James had often spoken to him of
me and my work, and apparently in a different
spirit from that which I had supposed him to
harbour for both. Possibly the whole trouble lay
in the dedication. I don't know. I only know that
from James himself I received no further letters—
not even an acknowledgement of the books I
continued to send him. For I thought it right to
do this whether he read them or not. I still regarded myself as his pupil, and deliberately
inserted a passage in *The Gentle Lover* as a sign of
my indebtedness. It was a close imitation of the
Master's later manner, but it was put there for
one purpose only—a purpose nevertheless un-
grasped by those who detected the passage.

Except for a favourable notice in *The Outlook*,
and another in the *Mercure de France*, *The Garden
God* was practically unreviewed. How it reached
the latter journal I cannot imagine, though I had
sent a copy to Anatole France, who now was on
the point of becoming, or perhaps had already
become, the prose writer I most admired. He
is also the writer to whom I owe most—in fact,
I sometimes feel, the only writer to whom I owe
anything. The influences of Pater and James were
bound to be transitory, because they did not
really suit me. The charm, the natural grace, the

simplicity and lucidity of France's style created a
new ideal, or revived an old one, a return to the
Greek spirit. I could not imitate that style, but
somehow it set me free to discover my own.

As for reviews, I had now reached a state of
mind when I thought the fewer there were the
better. A letter from Padraic Colum is in this
connection suggestive. I had seen a good deal of
Colum before I went to Cambridge. He was then
working on his play, *The Land*, and writing the
lyrics which later were published in the little
volume called *Wild Earth*. In fact, the poem,
Across the Door, was composed one morning on
the Antrim Road. It was too soon then for Colum
to decide whether it really was a poem or not, but
it was chanted experimentally into my ear, and
I knew that it was. The letter ran:

My dear Forrest Reid,

I'm very glad to have heard from you. I
would have written only I had a feeling you were
not at Cambridge and I awaited an address. I have
not yet got *The Garden God*. Griffiths got it and
gave it to Connolly. Connolly passed it on to
someone else as Griffiths would not publish a
review. It went up to Belfast. Connolly promises
he will get it for me in a day or two. I do not
know where to get a review in. Griffiths says the
book is "immoral", "morbid", or something.
Would it be worth while to get at *Uladh?* I had
a talk with Arthur Symons when I was in Lon-

don. He really likes *The Garden God*. He is very interested in you.

But Symons himself had already written to me, and his liking for the book did not mean that he found it orthodox. "Your rendering of a whole order of sentiment which is almost unintelligible to me forces my admiration, for you make it credible. The whole thing comes to be a kind of poem."

That was the point. I believed Symons to be a great critic, and I had tried, no doubt, to write a kind of poem, but not to render a whole order of sentiment which should be almost unintelligible. Nevertheless I could not help realizing by this time that to most persons it *must* be unintelligible, though surely a wide gulf separated the unintelligible from the immoral. If the story had been founded upon Christianity and not upon paganism, I should have judged the whole tone of *The Garden God* to be almost "pi". The intention behind the work was plain, and had immediately been perceived by its solitary French critic. "L'étrangeté du récit que Mr. Forrest Reid intitule: *The Garden God*, n'empêche pas d'en admirer la beauté. Cet épisode d'amour grec est enveloppé d'assez longues dissertations platoniciennes, et tout y est pur et absolument platonique." What, then, was all the fuss about? Very, very little. "And Jonathan told him, and said, I did but taste a little honey with the end of the rod that was in mine hand, and lo, I must die."

VI

CLOSE on these tiresome alarums came the visit to Cambridge of the Abbey players, accompanied by Yeats, Lady Gregory, Synge, and Padraic Colum. I took a week off and ran about all day with Colum, besides attending the nightly performances. The Abbey was then in its prime, and both plays and acting gave me more pleasure than any I have seen since. Also they awakened in me a kind of nostalgia for my own country. While I was living in Ireland I had taken Ireland very much for granted. Now, in an alien land, Yeats's *Cathleen Ni Houlihan* aroused in me an eager spirit of patriotism, the very existence of which I had not suspected. It was strange, because it wasn't in the least mixed up with politics. It was more like a family feeling—the feeling one has for brothers and sisters, which lies dormant and unrealized until an outsider perhaps says something in disparagement of them.

I had seen Yeats before, in London, but only for a moment, coming out of a theatre. Colum took me up to him now. He was standing alone, leaning against the wall, watching his own play, *On Baile's Strand*, and looking, as he always did, infinitely more distinguished than anybody else present. We stood, Colum and I, one on either side of him, and at intervals he kept murmuring, "Back into the melting pot; back into the melting pot," for he was not satisfied with his work. When the curtain descended Colum mentioned that I was writing an article on his early poetry, and suggested that it would be well if he were to tell me what to say. This was cheek, but of the kind Yeats liked, and he smiled gravely, and replied that I must think that out for myself. Colum told him that Symons had praised my book, and he shook his head slowly: "A great critic: a great critic." Then he signed his portrait for me—To Forest Reid from W. B. Yeats: but besides the mistake in spelling, the ink in his fountain pen ran out, and the collector in me watched uneasily and was dissatisfied. To Yeats, I found later, that particular instinct was incomprehensible: a book meant nothing to him apart from its contents. He did not possess even his own first editions. But then de la Mare is the same, and so is E. M. Forster. Like the compliment Henry James passed upon my handwriting, like my fondness for games, this collecting passion began to worry me a little. It evidently wasn't quite right, wasn't quite in order.

Synge I spoke to without any introduction, and I think it must have been at a rehearsal, for he was sitting half-way down the hall, with a bowler hat on, and rows of empty chairs on either side of him. In his isolation he looked, I thought, very much out of it. Yeats was the central figure, Lady Gregory was his prophet, Synge seemed to me neglected—and yet it was his plays and Lady

Gregory's that really made the show. He had none of Yeats's picturesqueness, none of the elfin charm of Colum: he looked stolid, ordinary, as if he might have been a banker or a stockbroker. I told him that his *Riders to the Sea* reminded me of Theocritos, which was true. He impressed me as being very simple, natural, and completely without vanity. At that time everybody was reading, or had read, *The Upton Letters*, which had been published anonymously, though of course the authorship was known at Cambridge. I hadn't read them and was uninterested. Synge hadn't read them, and apparently didn't want to, while at the same time feeling that he might be missing something. "Is it a book there is any necessity to read?" he asked, unluckily putting the question to A. C. Benson, who was its author. But Benson replied with perfect urbanity, "Not in the least." That is where the English have an advantage. Generations of the public-school tradition lay behind that "Not in the least".

This Irish invasion was a welcome interlude. Nightly, standing at the back of the hall beside Colum, I watched and listened to the Abbey players. And in the intervals, after his customary fashion, Colum would chant poetry into my ear.

> There's many a strong farmer
> Whose heart would break in two,
> If he could see the townland
> That we are riding to;
> Boughs have their fruit and blossom
> At all times of the year;

Rivers are running over
With red beer and brown beer.
An old man plays the bagpipes
In a golden and silver wood;
Queens, their eyes blue like the ice,
Are dancing in a crowd.

The little fox he murmured,
"O what of the world's bane?"
The sun was laughing sweetly,
The moon plucked at my rein;
But the little red fox murmured,
"O do not pluck at his rein,
He is riding to the townland
That is the world's bane."

That is not the version you will find in Yeats's
poems to-day, but it was the first version—the
version that I heard. It is odd how all my memories of Colum's conversation seem to pass
imperceptibly into lyrics—either his own or other
people's. I don't think anybody can ever have
cared more for poetry than he did, and he must
have known I liked it also, though I never quoted
it. I couldn't do it in his way; I was too self-
conscious; and I felt that any other way would be
wrong. He was then reading Dante in a translation, and he was also reading *The Ring and the Book*.
He read poets I couldn't read, and he nearly always had a volume in his pocket. And everything he read he seemed straightway to know by
heart, whether he had liked it or not. If he told
you So-and-so was a bad poet, he would immediately quote one of his poems from memory to

show you how bad he was. It was a marvellous gift—more akin to an ear for music than anything else. Not long ago, just outside the City Hall here in Belfast, I heard a young street sweeper whistling "Ah! fors' è lui", with all its runs and trills, its elaborate *coloratura*, in perfect tune from start to finish. I could not resist questioning him, and found that he did not know what it was; simply he had heard it in a cinema the night before, sung by some operatic soprano. One hardly expects this kind of thing outside Italy, but Colum had a similar gift for remembering verse.

VII

AFTER *The Garden God*, with the exception of one or two articles, my writing came temporarily to a standstill. At Cambridge I was much too busy to start on another novel. Occasionally I jotted down an idea, but I felt that these seeds were unlikely to germinate. André Raffalovich had written urging me to do a novel about the youth of Beckford. This, he seemed to think, would be an ideal subject for me, and his letter was accompanied by Lewis Melville's biography, which he admitted was extremely unsatisfactory. I read the biography and could see that, despite its contradictions, evasions, and ambiguities, it contained a subject; but obviously there were pitfalls as well, and a great deal of preliminary spade work would be necessary. In fact, the more I pondered the thing, the more difficult it appeared. At present, of course, it was quite impossible to tackle it, but even had I been free the task still would have remained daunting. I read all Beckford's published works, except *Azemia*, and *Modern Novel Writing* (both unobtainable); but there were private writings, too, one ought to consult, unless everything was to be imagined, in which case why cling to historical accuracy at all? Yes, it was difficult, one would have to steep oneself in the period; and though I felt strongly drawn to the experiments in magic, there was the ordinary everyday life lived on a scale far too princely for me to hope to picture it successfully. Beckford himself I thought I could do; and the mysterious William, and the dabblings in magic, but——

Since the publication of Mr. Guy Chapman's study I now see more than ever that there *is* a subject there, and a most fascinating one (the music lessons given by the infant prodigy Mozart to his still more infantile pupil would certainly be one of my chapters), but I trust nobody will treat it who is not in sympathy with its astonishing hero; and what, I suppose, tempted me was that I *was* in sympathy—at any rate with the love of nature, the love of animals, the love of music, the friendship theme, the interest in magic.

After funking Beckford it may seem surprising that without any outside encouragement I actually began to take notes for a novel about Chatterton, and even went so far as to visit his native haunts in search of local colour. More surprising still, I dare say, were the notes for a purely imaginative Life of Christ—the scene laid in a romantic pastoral country—the drama arising out of the conflict between paganism and Christianity, and ending with the death of Pan. I must confess I rather fancied this work; but since it became more and more pagan, more and more fantastic, and less and less Christian as it proceeded, I abandoned it too.

Now while I was at Cambridge these false starts

did not really matter, but after I came down I began to feel a little uneasy, for it seemed to me clear that if I really were going to be a novelist the first step must be to write a novel, and my steps at present were not leading to much. I have been glancing through the letters I wrote to Theo Bartholomew at this time, and they are filled with allusions to books I never wrote, and whose very subjects I have forgotten. At last, through sheer determination, I composed *A Romantic Experiment*—a full-length ordinary novel with the ordinary love interest—very ordinary indeed. I sent it to Theo and his criticism was guarded—so guarded that when the typescript came back I read the thing again and destroyed it. I liked the title, but all the rest was flat as stale beer.

Meanwhile James Rutherford and I were living at Newcastle, County Down—between the mountains and the sea. James had been received into the church, and was waiting for an appointment; Andrew had forsaken the law for medicine; the third brother, Willie, had abandoned the idea of the church and had gone to Cambridge to read for the History Tripos. It seemed to me that we were all taking an unconscionably long time in finding our proper grooves. James had started as an engineer; Andrew and I had started in the tea-trade; Willie first had intended to be a missionary, next a parson, and now was planning to be a schoolmaster: surely all this chopping and changing was unusual. So, for that matter, was the bond between us, which was close, and based on something underlying and outweighing extraordinary temperamental differences.

It was on an autumn afternoon, at the Newcastle tennis club, that I suddenly conceived the idea for a new book. There were several schoolboys there, and James and I made up a four with two of them. My partner was called "Skinny" by his companions, but his name was Denis, and he struck me as a remarkably pleasant person. I had no more talk with him than one has when playing foursomes—the inevitable "Sorry!", or, more rarely, "Oh, well played, partner!"—nevertheless the brief encounter gave my imagination just the fillip it needed, and that evening, when I went home, I blocked out a synopsis of *The Moon Story*.

This, at least, was how I planned it originally—a fantastic and lyrical tale, no longer than *The Garden God*. But before I started on the actual writing I changed my plan. The process which had transformed *The Garden God* from a realistic school story into a lyrical romance was now exactly reversed. *This* lyrical romance I decided to turn into a realistic novel, still keeping the moon story as a subsidiary theme, but introducing more characters, and treating the whole thing as a family chronicle. When it was finished I called it *The Bracknels*. I sent it to Edward Arnold, whom I chose because, the year before, he had published de la Mare's *The Return*.

It was accepted, but on the condition that I

should add a further chapter or two. This I did; and to those interested I may mention that the book originally ended on what is now page 289, with the words, "I don't know how we are to tell her." It was the kind of ending I liked—tragic yet indeterminate—and it was with extreme reluctance that I carried the tale on for three more chapters. Yet E. M. F. says Arnold was right— so perhaps he was. It is a book I should like to revise—it and *The Spring Song*, and possibly *Pirates*—bringing all three into tune with *Apostate* and its successors, as I did in the case of *Following Darkness*.

Twenty years later I met, and again on a sports ground, though this time it was in England, the "onlie begetter" of *The Bracknels*, who in the meantime had become an officer in the British Army, and was no longer called "Skinny". My momentary reaction was, I confess, one of surprise, almost indignation, but I swiftly recovered from this. I wondered if by any chance he had read the book, though even if he had, there was nothing he could recognize, for the entire story was an imagination, and its characters gathered from the four winds. Yet *The Bracknels*—or the Moon Story in it—was the first of my tales that seemed to me to come out of a mysterious region of "other" reality. So, later, came *Uncle Stephen* and *The Retreat*. One knows, I mean, when one invents a story or a character, and one knows when these are the products of direct observation.

But the particular tales I have in mind fall into neither category. Where did my moon-worshipper come from? He was not consciously invented, certainly not observed; he was created by a collaborator working beneath consciousness, of whom I may have more to say when his influence becomes more paramount.

In the meantime any reference I make to these early books can be taken for what it is—a memory, an impression; I have not re-read them, because the conception alone, not what I made of it, is relevant to the present chronicle. My impression, then, of *The Bracknels* is that its texture must be broken, uneven, that the various members of the family were drawn from sources too widely separated to be united convincingly *as* a family. Some attempt to solve this problem I did make, no doubt, in my choice of the father and the mother. I was very scientific here, or hoped I was. The father was to account for Alfred and Amy, the mother for May and Denis, while, if this were not going too far, the ill-assorted union itself for the spiritual life of Denis. And I am not sure that it *is* going too far. One remembers Shelley and *his* father. I very much prefer Denis to Shelley, but the contrast between father and son is equally marked in both cases, and in both the natural antagonism helps to account for some of the son's peculiarities.

The Bracknels, if I am not mistaken, had a fairly good press. At all events, no exception was taken to it as had been to *The Garden God*, though I need hardly say that the writer's point of view was unaltered. Perhaps there was something in the broader treatment, or in the setting of everyday life, or in the introduction of "intelligible sentiment" (poor Amy's, I'm afraid), that rendered it more acceptable and less liable to misinterpretation.

As for the background—the lovely Lagan valley, the river itself, the house, the woods—all these, I think *must* be there, *must* come through; for they had been my world from childhood, and were the kind of thing I found easiest to do. It may be objected that what comes most easily is not always, in the result, what proves most successful. This is so, but as I said before I am only recording the impression that remains with me: nothing could be further from my desire and intention than to suggest a critical judgement, even were it fitting or possible for me to do so.

VIII

IN chapter X of *Apostate* I have described a dream-place that was familiar to me in my childhood and boyhood, and a dream-companion. The writing of *The Garden God* was in a sense a pursuit of this dream, though the story itself is not what I mean by a dream story. Some of my later tales were literally dream stories; that is to say, they were composed in sleep; but I shall not touch on these at present, for I am trying to follow a chronological sequence.

The Garden God, then, we may describe simply as a first and very tentative effort to treat the friendship theme, and when I took this theme up again five years later in *The Bracknels*, several differences are to be noted. To begin with, it is no longer a "solitary song" with an accompaniment of Platonic reflections and divagations, but is mingled with other themes, other interests and influences, the naturalistic form is accepted, and the whole thing is brought into touch with actual life. Secondly, the friends are no longer contemporaries, playmates, children building castles on the shores of time. It is the difference between a drama and a lyric. The relationship itself is much more complicated, has ceased to be a mere wish-fulfilment, and the characters are conceived realistically. It follows from this that what the older friend, the tutor, gives is not exactly the same as what he receives. The protective element has grown much stronger; there is a sense of responsibility, a moral significance, where before there was only the instinctive affection of children, and hence the entire story strikes a deeper note. Rusk's affection for his pupil is charged with anxiety; it is unselfish; he wants to do everything he can for him, and though he fails, it is not because his affection fails. The failure comes through a weakness of imagination: the friends are not equal, and it is the younger friend who is the more intelligent, the more imaginative, the more sensitive. The tutor can do nothing for him in the hour of danger, because he cannot really understand him. He feels his own helplessness; he blunders and stumbles, and perseveres; but he is fighting against an invisible enemy who watches and waits, and when the hour has come strikes.

The creed accepted, accepted from Socrates, and never to be abandoned, is that the only thing we *can* love is the good. "Fate which has ordained that there shall be no friendship among the evil has also ordained that there shall ever be friendship among the good."

This was what I believed, and is what I still believe. Pico della Mirandola, it is said, kept in his study a lamp burning continually before the bust of Plato. I had hung a portrait of Socrates on my wall. It was Socrates, not Plato, who was to me the living figure. And if I myself, after more than two thousand years, could come under the influence of his charm and wisdom, it was easy to understand the affection and devotion that direct personal contact with him must have inspired. The half-bantering manner, the irony which could be so deadly a weapon when it encountered intellectual arrogance, could also be sweet as honey when he liked, and certainly it was one of the fascinations that drew to him all that was finest in the youth of Athens. Nevertheless, I suspect that it was, too, partly responsible for the later tragedy. Or rather a clumsy imitation of it, devoid of grace, devoid of playfulness, devoid of charm. You see, in my own boyhood, I myself imitated it—when I could draw anybody into an argument concerning ethics or religion. The effect, I need scarcely add, proved anything but endearing. But human nature does not change much, therefore I feel sure that it was imitated in ancient Greece by eager young disciples, fresh from the delightful entertainment afforded by the discomfiture of a Thrasymachos or a Euthyphro. And no doubt it would be practised at home— and probably on indignant parents. It becomes therefore easy to see why an enthusiasm for Socrates was not always shared by the older generation. For little could be done about it. Much of Greek life was lived out of doors, and out of doors Socrates was always there, like the weather, and always surrounded by a ring of embryo philosophers.

He had a genius for friendship, and it did not

take the form of a narrow attachment to a single individual, but flowed out freely in every direction. I don't think I exaggerate in saying that nobody can ever have lived a life that more perfectly suited him. Even that last scene, when he drank the hemlock, surrounded by his pupils, can hardly be called unhappy. It was sad—yes—but there were none of the ravages of disease, none of the weaknesses of old age, death itself approached painlessly, and he met it firmly convinced that the separation from his friends would be but brief. Xanthippe had been led weeping away. Fate, I feel, has been a little unkind to Xanthippe. She has, perhaps quite unjustly, come down the ages as a shrew. Plato, indeed, speaks no ill of her; she does not interest him; yet even Plato in that final scene somehow does manage to suggest that, though others may have wept, Xanthippe, like poor Mrs. Wix in *What Maisie Knew*, "was the only one who made a noise".

However, I am not writing an essay on Socrates. He came in, I suspect, because he is the only historical figure who shares for me something of the warmth and actuality of those I have known in the flesh. From my first discovery of him—that is to say from the time when I was seventeen or eighteen—I had come under his spell. He possessed every virtue I was most in sympathy with, and therefore most admired. For though we may accept, we can never truly appreciate or love, what lies outside our comprehension,

and our comprehension is strictly conditioned and
limited by temperament. I could imagine nobody
wiser or better than Socrates, but none the less he
belonged to, was in my world. All the dangers
that encompassed me were dangers he himself had
felt and understood and conquered. He represented an ideal, and the very knowledge that there
once had been such a man meant much, even
though I doubted if there had ever been another
comparable to him. A. E. found his ideal in the
Eastern mystics; Andrew, even after he had
abandoned Christianity, still found his ideal in the
Gospels; but I required something more human,
something closer to the earth. To Socrates the
beauty of the earth, and the beauty of youth in all
its gaiety and happiness, foreshadowed the beauty
of heaven. He was infinitely approachable; he met
Lysis and his peers on their own ground; and if
presently they were contemplating eternity the
human touch was never lost. Possibly I am giving
too scanty credit here to the art of Plato, for it is
due to that art that Lysis and his friends *are* boys,
that Socrates himself lives, when he might have
been as dull and prosaic a puppet as the Socrates
of Xenophon. But Plato later was to repudiate
that kind of art, and with it all the geniality and
warmth and affection and humour which his early
portait of Socrates demanded. In the end he was
obliged to abandon Socrates himself, for there
was no use in attributing to him the arid ratio-
cination of *The Laws*. So we get, in exchange, an

Athenian Stranger. But the Athenian Stranger remains a cypher. There is no faintest attempt to breathe into him the breath of life; he is a ghost in a grey wintry world; the heart of the artist seems to have withered as the memory of his master and friend grew dim. I even believe that the real Socrates was more wonderful and lovable than Plato's presentment of him. Nevertheless, this in itself proves how supreme that portrait is as a testimony of admiration and love. For it is nearly impossible not to give all that is best, certainly all that is most delightful, in Plato to Socrates. And if we do so, it is no more than what Plato himself desired—yet it cannot be the whole truth. Nobody but a Greek could have risen to such a task so nobly, with so complete a self-effacement. To realize *how* complete it is we have but to compare it with a masterpiece of a later day—with Boswell's *Johnson*.

IX

HERE is a true story, more than a hundred years old, gleaned from a far too long, most uneven, but occasionally charming book, *The Doctor*, by Robert Southey. A troop of British cavalry which had served on the continent was disbanded in the City of York, and the horses were put up for sale. The troop's commander, however, Sir Robert Clayton, was a rich man. So, because he disliked the idea of these old equine warriors being worked to death as hacks, he bought them himself, and at the same time bought a part of Knavesmire Heath, where he turned them loose to pass a comfortable and leisurely old age. It was, I think, the natural act of a gentleman, and was remembered chiefly because of a strange thing that happened later. On one occasion, when the horses were scattered grazing here and there on the heath, a summer storm gathered, and presently the first lightnings flashed, and the first thunders began to roll. Then, taking these fires and sounds to be the signal of approaching battle, the horses were seen to get together of their own accord, and form a perfect line to meet the enemy, just as if their old masters were on their backs.

Now, though I might be at a loss to explain why, I somehow find this story oddly touching. Perhaps it is because the qualities of innocence and faithfulness are in it, and these are qualities

94

that I happen to place very, very high, and to have found, alas! much more the property of beasts than of humans. *You* may see only the mechanical result of habit and training, but if so, upon this point we can never be in agreement, and I had better warn you that the whole of the ensuing chapter is going to be about animals. To me they are important, and my life would have been a poor and meagre thing without them. In the same book, *The Doctor*, we read that one John Henderson "saw the spirit of a slumbering cat pass from her in pursuit of a visionary mouse". I have no such fantastical experience to record, but I am convinced, by the very fact that animals dream at all— and no intelligent observer will deny this—that imagination is not an exclusively human gift. Every cat, I expect, has dreamed of mice and birds, for these are wish-fulfilment dreams, and cats, therefore, would be particularly liable to them. Also all animal dreams probably are very direct and simple, offering no scope to the egregious and unconvincing Freud; but into the dreams of a dog, I should think, his master, and indeed every member of the particular human family he happens to be looking after, quite frequently enter.

In November, while I was at work on *The Bracknels*, James and I came back to Belfast and took a house in South Parade, not far from Newtownbreda Presbyterian Church, to which he

had been appointed as assistant to the Reverend
Doctor Workman. It was one of those old-
fashioned terrace houses, now fast disappearing,
with a small garden in front, consisting of a row
of iron railings, plenty of slugs and snails, a
straggling hedge, a plot of feeble grass through
which the soil showed, and a single fuliginous
shrub of gloomy and forbidding appearance.
Nothing else would grow in that garden, but the
shrub maintained a dogged existence until in the
end I cut it down.

The household consisted of Minnie—a maid
we had had before my mother's death—of James
and myself, of a bulldog called Pan, an Irish
terrier called Nyx, and a cat called Pussy. One
observes a lack of originality in this last, but
except for purposes of fiction the christening of
cats has always seemed to me superfluous. A dog
is extremely conscious of his name, and though
he be dozing will cock an ear and half open an
eye if he hears it mentioned in the most casual
conversation, but cats are not even faintly
interested, and since they respond to anything
when in responsive mood, and to nothing when
feeling unresponsive, the generic "puss" suffices.

Nevertheless, the eternal feline in this particular
puss, through constant rubbing shoulders with
dogs underwent some slight modification. I
fancied I even detected a certain disappointment
when she produced a family of kittens, not
puppies. At any rate she produced no second

family, and though this may have been due to accident, she received full credit for it, and universal applause.

In order of seniority she came first; then Pan; then Nyx; and for a while there were no further additions. Pan was only a few weeks old when I got him. He could not manage stairs; a tap of the cat's paw would send him sprawling. It had been the dream of my boyhood to possess a bulldog, and now that I had one, though he may have been taken too soon from his mother and brothers and sisters, I think he had a fairly good time. What was unexpected was the interest the cat took in him from the beginning. This was all the stranger because she took no interest in Nyx whatever. She lived beside Nyx for years without betraying a consciousness of his existence, but Pan she could not leave alone, though her first conception of him, doubtless, was as a kind of mechanical toy. When I was writing or reading he was usually in the same armchair with me, sprawled across my knees. The cat would wait until the first sighing snores grew deeper, then, like a shadow, she would descend from her chair, and glide noiselessly beneath mine. Presently a paw would come up between my legs and Pan would be scratched gently on the stomach. A deep growl would follow, but no movement: then another scratch, and this time he would open his eyes in indignation, knowing perfectly well who was there. It was distinctly comic, for the cat knew that I knew and would not interfere. I do not wish to exaggerate, but there is surely something here approximating to a sense of humour. A little boy's very primitive humour of course, finding expression in mischief, teasing, and practical jokes, but that Puss was amused I am convinced.

This domestic life was very interesting to watch as it developed; the three temperaments being so entirely different. The cat and the bull-dog probably were happier than the terrier, because they were not jealous. Puss was not jealous, because she did not care enough; Pan because he had nothing to be jealous about. Nyx perhaps had—at least to the extent that he was never so great a pet. James used to reproach me for this, the petting being regarded as my business. But then he was not a pettable dog: he would growl if you lifted him, and he would not sit in the same chair with you, though, as I was to learn later, he was the most faithful little soul imaginable. For when James got married he took Nyx with him to Warrenpoint, and for a year or two I did not see him. But when we did meet again, when he heard my step in the hall, though he was now old, crippled with rheumatism, and nearly blind, he welcomed me with so much agitation that I had straightway to flop on the floor and clasp him in my arms till the emotion of the first greeting should be over. It filled me with the bitterest remorse, when I thought of how much more I had always made of Pan and Remus. And I remem-

bered the dog Argos in the *Odyssey*, who alone
recognized the returned wanderer. "He wagged
his tail and raised both his ears, but nearer to
his master he had not now strength to draw."
Homer is not sentimental, he does not elaborate
the incident, but like all the Greeks he loved
and understood animals, and the strength and
unchangeableness of their affection. Odysseus,
though pretty tough in most ways, is moved to
tears; then he passes on into the house. "But
upon Argos came the black fate of death even in
the hour that he beheld Odysseus again, after the
twentieth year." The passage is peculiarly Greek;
it is as natural in Homer as it would be unnatural
in a Bible story or in one of the epics of Milton.
I suppose Nyx thought I had been good to him:
I felt that I had not been nearly good enough. He
was a collector too—of ancient bones, which he
kept hidden under the sacking and pine-shavings
that composed his bed. I used to come upon his
collection when I was remaking the bed, and,
having a fellow feeling, was always careful to
replace it intact. Pan and James did not collect.

Pan was fond of games—particularly of tug-of-
war played with an old pair of trousers—but he
had no hunting instincts; Nyx would kill a cat or a
hen if he got the chance. He was at once pug-
nacious, nervous, and extraordinarily courageous
—a combination that inevitably makes for trouble.
It was partly, no doubt, the feeling that he had
the bulldog behind him which gave him confi-

dence, for I have seen him offering battle to an Irish wolfhound about five times his size. Fortunately the wolfhound was young and good-natured, and merely knocked him over and placed a paw upon him till I was able to come to the rescue; but the number of unintentional, ill-directed dog-bites I have received is astonishing, and I bear the marks of several of them to this day.

Pan, on the other hand, was distinctly peaceable. Yet it was Pan I should have relied upon for protection: it was he who, in a railway carriage, when a friend of mine entered with a rather too boisterous greeting, instantly appeared from under the seat, so that the greeting faded into a frozen immobility. I cannot deny that the incident pleased me. There was something about that quiet emergence far more effective than the excitement of Nyx would have been. There was no bark, no growl, and yet one felt that neither would there be any hesitation. So I made one or two encouraging and slightly patronizing remarks to my friend, explained his rather impetuous entrance to Pan, and the incident closed.

The cat, as I have said, while ignoring Nyx completely, had bullied Pan when he was small, but attempted to form an alliance with him when he grew larger. Her methods were boldly feminine. At meal times, when naturally he had to be on the alert, she would stalk to and fro before him, with tail erect, arching her back just when it came beneath his chin so that she might brush against him, while he held his face averted in visible distaste. And when he was sufficiently drowsy she would get into the same chair with him, and a picture of intense affection would be presented, though the affection on one side consisted of somnolence, and on the other of a desire for warm snuggling comfort. There were certain things, however, that she definitely might not do, and one of these was to share bones. There was nearly always an abandoned bone lying about, gnawed and licked by both dogs until it was meatless and polished as a billiard ball. Yet this treasure evidently could still arouse desire. The cat would wait until the dogs seemed wrapped in slumber, and then, with infinite precaution, approach the bone. What, with her small teeth and jaws, she expected to accomplish I don't know, for the performance was never allowed to proceed very far. Through dreams, a sense of the impending profanation would mysteriously reach the sleepers, and there would be a simultaneous horrified awakening, two pounces, a swirl, and next moment the offender would be on the table or a bookcase. I dare say I might have modified these unwritten taboos, but after all there were few of them and they were amusing. Another ban, I remember, was against sneezing—a habit to which cats, unlike dogs, happen to be rather prone. To sneeze was a signal for instant attack, so the cat sneezed as seldom as possible.

Later we moved into a more attractive house
in Fitzwilliam Avenue. Here my bedroom was at
the top of the house, Pan had a special kennel
built for him in the yard, while the cat, Nyx, and
James, all slept in one room on the ground floor.
Nyx had his bed in a corner, composed of
sacking and pine-shavings; the cat slept at the foot
of James's bed for the first part of the night, and
towards morning stretched herself across his neck,
or, if it were chilly, got under the bedclothes.
This bed was drawn up beside the window, and
over the bottom sash, which was always left open,
was a wire netting containing an aperture just
sufficiently large for the cat to go in and out. For,
unlike the dogs, she lived an independent life, and
her hours were irregular. In the long run she
always did return to snatch forty winks before
daylight, but nobody ever knew exactly when, her
entries and exits being discreet and silent, un-
remarked even by Nyx. Yet there came a night
when I was awakened by the most terrific din
conceivable. To reach me it had had to penetrate
two ceilings and an intervening room, but reach
me it did. Returning in the small hours, the cat
had been accompanied by a friend. She, of course,
knew where her private door was, and the friend,
following closely, had plunged after her into the
inky blackness beyond, little guessing what it
contained. It contained the sleeping James, which
did not much matter, but it contained also the
astonished and outraged Nyx, no cat fancier at

any time. To retreat, to find again the hole in the netting, was impossible, and an air-raid would have been dreamily soporific compared with the hunt which now took place in the darkness. I couldn't even imagine what was happening—apparently an attack of some sort, in which lives were being sold dearly. By the time I reached the scene the light of course was on, but the room was a litter of glass, china, and photograph frames, with the lover crouched on the top of a chest of drawers, and Nyx frantically attempting to join him there. *Our* cat had gone to bed.

This detachment of cats, this absolute indifference to all that does not immediately concern the particular desire of the moment, is something both superhuman and supercanine. A few weeks later I was to witness a still more striking example of it, when, on returning from a walk, we saw Puss in the garden with what may or may not have been the same friend. Everything happened in a flash, and before Nyx could be checked the stranger, his spine broken, lay dead at his dear one's feet. And—will you believe it?—that dear one never stirred an inch from where she was seated, but putting up a languid paw began to wash her face. We took the corpse into the house, and at night brought it out again and buried it secretly. For we had recognized it. Old Doctor Rose, who lived opposite, made enquiries about his cat, to whom he was much attached, but old Doctor Rose never learned the truth. I do not mean that he was told lies: on the other hand, he was certainly left in the gardens of illusion: cats come and cats go: this one, we definitely knew, had gone for ever; but it seemed kinder not to say so.

James was fond of animals, though being an ardent humanitarian, not perhaps quite in the way I was. At times he complained that the study smelt like a zoo, and at times undoubtedly it did do so. Also he thought me messy in my habit of attending to the dogs with my own hands, and not washing them immediately afterwards. Yet one can't be always washing one's hands. I admit I am less fastidious concerning animals than concerning humans. In fact *much* less fastidious. It does not disgust me to remove with my fingers the secretion that gathers in the corners of a cow's eyes, attracts flies, and must cause the cow discomfort. James thought this messy.

Then, in an unlucky hour, we decided to increase the family by getting a monkey. When I was a little boy, the monkeys who accompanied piano-organs and ear-ringed Italians used to rack me with sympathy and compassion. I wanted to adopt them, after the fashion of Stevie in *The Secret Agent*. I was sure those smiling bland Italians illtreated them, just as I was sure that the bear who was dragged round the streets by an odious person with an accordion was illtreated by *him*. And so, when an advertisement of a young marmoset for sale appeared in *Exchange and Mart*, I answered it, and two or three days later, in a wooden case labelled "monkey with care", the marmoset arrived. It arrived in the early winter afternoon, and we carried the case upstairs to the study to open it. Pan and Nyx and Pussy were all present; the box was placed on the hearthrug; in the grate a cheerful fire was burning; I felt quite excited as I removed the front of the cage. And the first thing that wretched monkey did was to jump into the very middle of the cheerful fire. He did not stay there long; in a second he was out and had streaked up a curtain, from which he swung himself to the top of one of the bookcases. It was James's bookcase, a theological bookcase, and the monkey remained perched there, his bright eyes shining in a strangely ancient and wrinkled face as he peered down at us. What surprised me was that the dogs seemed entirely uninterested. Pan merely climbed as usual into his armchair, and Nyx turned his back. Only Pussy, crouching on the hearthrug, her tail switching ominously, stared fixedly at the visitor with green unblinking eyes. So we remained till the monkey, for some foolish reason, descended from the top of the bookcase to the next shelf. Naturally the space here was narrow, but with one thin black hand clutching Barnes on *Ephesians*, he managed to balance himself precariously. Then Barnes began to yield. Slowly yet visibly— distressingly visibly. It was but a matter of seconds, and not many of these. Out came Barnes, and down came Barnes and monkey with a bang.

In one single leap the cat was on his back, the claws of her fore-paws dug into his neck, her hind legs working like piston-rods and sending out showers of fur. Round and round the room they tore before a rescue could be effected, the monkey screaming, the cat silent. Yet we had never even contemplated danger from this quarter. In discussion it had always been—How would the monkey get on with the dogs? or How would the dogs get on with the monkey?—questions that to this day remain unanswered. James got a new home for the monkey that afternoon, and later we learned that the advertisement had been a lying one. The monkey was old, had never been a pet, had obviously been kept all his life in a cage— which at least helped to explain his leap into the fire.

Discouraged by this failure, we did not repeat the experiment. It was clear that the cat drew the line at monkeys, and yet it annoyed me to think that we had to accept her ruling. The dogs never would have behaved in this fashion. They had loyalties, they had consciences, they did not take action on the impulse of the moment, with the possibility that that action might be all wrong. I once found poor old Pan blowing a terrified mouse all round the room, but without attempting to injure it. He was merely investigating; the mouse *might* be a new pet. But the cat had no such scruples and would growl furiously if you took a bird from her. On one occasion I had to chase her all over the house before I was able to rescue a sparrow she had captured, and if she had been anything approaching my own size she wouldn't have given it up then. But I took it out of her mouth—a dead bird apparently, though I could find no trace of injury. So I placed it on a sheet of cotton-wool, on the window-sill in the sun, and in a quarter of an hour, perhaps, it suddenly revived and flew away as if nothing had happened.

The cat had not only no moral sense, she even played the part of tempter to the others. On Christmas day James and I were called out in the middle of dinner to speak to somebody, and though we were not gone for more than two or three minutes, when we returned we saw an empty dish, no turkey. The turkey was beneath the table, and Pan and Nyx were mounting guard over it, but not touching it. This was the cat's work. She had handed it down, and they had refused to become her accomplices.

Pan had a good many names: Nyx, I think, had only two—Nyx and Doctor. The latter was derived from *The Second Mrs. Tanqueray*, which, owing to my admiration for Mrs. Patrick Campbell, I had been to see four times in one week. "Doctor! Frank!" It was Aubrey Tanqueray's appeal to his bachelor friends, as he explains at a farewell supper his peculiar position to them, and somehow, in a burlesque form, it appealed to the dogs. For dogs like being talked to, and the quality of the conversation—its wisdom or foolishness—doesn't very much matter, because they create their own meaning from it, as I do from the words in Italian opera. I talked a lot to Pan, and later to Remus, another bulldog, and later still to Roger, who was a sheepdog. I remember, one day, when I was unhappy, Roger very nearly talked to me. Looking back at them—and it is only when one looks back that one sees clearly—I am inclined to believe that these canine friendships were more successful, and certainly far less disappointing ultimately, than any human relationships I have ever achieved. They were not perfect; there was no discussion of ideas; on the other hand there was no failure, no change.

I never wrote about Nyx, I never wrote about Roger, but I wrote about Pan in *Following Darkness*, and Remus in *The Spring Song*. I gave them other names. I called Pan "Tony", and Remus "Pouncer". Pouncer was a good name, but Tony wasn't, so when I rewrote the book as *Peter Waring* I changed it. With the wrong name I can make no headway. The cat in *The Retreat* is called Henry simply because Henry was for me the right name; in actual life he was called Danny. He was not my cat. I stayed with him once for a fortnight, and on a later occasion he stayed for a fortnight with me. But it was in his own house that most of his exploits took place and that he worked his magics. These, on the whole, I reported faithfully, with, as Huckleberry Finn would say, "some stretchers", but not many—really, as such things go, surprisingly few.

I got Remus, my second bulldog, at a dog show in Leeds. I went over for that special purpose, crossing one night and returning on the next. The pups had not yet been put into the ring when I made my choice, but I was indifferent to the judge's ruling, and though Remus was only awarded second prize, it was he who accompanied me back to Ireland. In the train we had a carriage to ourselves, and long before we reached Liverpool had become confidential. On board the steamer, I took him down to the kitchen and discussed the situation with the cook. I knew there would be no difficulty, because bulldogs, though they inspire timidity in the timid, are at the same time extraordinarily popular. With men, that is to say: women, except those of the sporting, open-air type, for some reason seem to find them less attractive.

The kitchen was warm and pleasant—far pleasanter, I decided, than my poky little cabin— and we soon fixed up a bed in the cosiest corner. The next question was, Would the traveller be seasick? This we discussed, and it was the cook who suggested that half a glass of brandy in some warm milk might be a stomach-settler. I was more doubtful, but the stomach-settler was lapped up, and I was told in the morning that it had been quite, or very nearly quite, successful.

My memories of Pan and Remus have with time become very much intermingled, which is odd, because, though in their relation to me there was no difference, in some other respects there was a marked difference between them. Pan was mild; Remus had the blood of bull-baiting ancestors in his veins; and this was revealed from the beginning. Its earliest manifestation, I confess, was more absurd than alarming. I don't know whether the old street-sweeping machines still exist or not. I fancy not; but they consisted in a long cylindrical brush that revolved on wheels when drawn, as it invariably was, by an elderly horse, who, like most Corporation workers, did not believe in haste. The average speed of these contraptions might be perhaps a quarter of a mile an hour; nevertheless Remus, within a week of his arrival, was run over by one. Then indeed arose lamentations! The horse heard them and stopped immediately, seizing the opportunity to step on to the footpath and pluck some mouthfuls from a hedge. So there we were—I consoling the cry-baby, the horse wrenching sprays from the hedge, the driver good-naturedly apologetic. The only sufferer was Remus himself, and I fondly hoped it might be a lesson to him. But it wasn't; nothing could cure him; he would fly at the throat of any animal sufficiently large; and in spite of the most careful watching, more than once he nearly got me into serious trouble. True, Pan had perhaps brought me nearer still—the innocent and benevolent Pan, confronted by a white and furious gamekeeper with raised and pointed gun. "If that dog takes one step forward I'll shoot him." Fortunately the step was not taken.

Neither Pan nor Remus lived to be old dogs. About a year after Pan's death I got Remus, and that was wise; but when Remus died I was too much upset to think he could ever have a successor. I have mentioned Roger, but Roger came many years later, and though he spent his days with me he was not, strictly speaking, my dog, and returned at night to his owners. Sometimes he returned reluctantly, but after all I couldn't very well take complete possession of him, and it didn't really much matter whether he slept in their house or mine. With Roger therefore it was a case of friendship, and this friendship was established without any preliminary advances on my part. At least I can remember none: my first recollection is of two fore-paws suddenly planted in the middle of my back while I was kneeling down, weeding a flower bed: Roger had called to propose a walk. I was pleased and flattered, for he was a mature and middle-aged dog. Also he was the cleverest dog I have ever known. Pan and Remus were not particularly clever, but a word to Roger was sufficient. If I told him I was going into town and could not take him with me, he would be disappointed, but make no attempt to accompany me. On the other hand, twice when I went out in the evening to play bridge and forgot to send him home, I found him at midnight still waiting patiently for me on the doorstep. Yet those hours of waiting must have been abysmally dull. And all the time he was within a few hundred yards of his own home, while the sole pleasure he had to look forward to was the very short walk back.

I must add here that there was one house I visited, though only one—Ballyhackamore House, belonging to the Montgomeries—where all my views about animals were shared. Mrs Montgomery was, I think, the gentlest and sweetest old lady I have ever met. Latterly she was an invalid and confined to one large room on the ground floor—the drawing-room really, though her bed had been brought down to it. And I have gone in to see her, and found a vigorous young rooster perched on the back of her chair, a polecat in her lap, a blind old dog slumbering at her feet, and a pony looking in at the window. Naturally this was a room I liked, and these visits had something of the quality of the golden age about them. Mrs. Montgomery herself talked little, but that did not seem to matter. She produced upon me an impression of goodness, absolute goodness, that was strangely peaceful. There was no question here of religion, of conscientiousness, of duty; it was the real thing, pure, unmixed, a natural gift. I never heard her passing an unfavourable remark about anybody, and I cannot even imagine her doing so. It was with infinite reluctance, and because it was forced upon her, that she once reproached me with certain laxities of style—the use of "and which", for instance, the ending of a sentence with a preposition—but it seemed more a caress than a criticism, and the trouble it caused her made me laugh.

In Ballyhackamore House even mice were sacred. No traps might be set, and if a mouse were discovered (naturally they had grown bold), he was conducted out at the back door, and who can blame him if he promptly returned by the front. This, I may say, actually did happen, unless the mouse who entered was a twin brother.

Desmond, the grandson, aged ten or eleven, sometimes sent me a note when he was going to be there, so that I might drop in. We played cricket in the big yard, and later on, in the evening, played cards with Granny and Aunt Betty. Granny was not very good at cards, and since her grandson was extremely frank in pointing out mistakes these games used to amuse me intensely. It was with Desmond that I built the bonfire I have described in *The Retreat*—a bonfire that even set a brick wall burning. It was a glorious show, but as it increased in glory anxious messages began to arrive from the house, and presently we had to beat it out.

Desmond was just the kind of boy I liked—toughish, self-reliant, fond of animals, and the best of pals—therefore it seemed to me very strange that he and his grandfather did not get on well together. For they didn't. Yet what did the old man want? I could not understand it, but the grandfather appeared even to resent the notice I took of "that ill-mannered brat", as he called him. Of course, he was alarmingly literary, I was supposed to be there to talk to him about books, and, that I should prefer to play games with

H   113

a small boy, I'm afraid annoyed him. He would cast ever more baleful glances at his grandson, hover on the verge of dismissing him, and in the end stalk off in disgust to another room. Then Granny would murmur an excuse, but I knew that secretly she was on our side. Unfortunately, on one of these manifestations I also knew that the window of the study whither Grandfather presumably had retired had been cracked that afternoon during cricket practice, though we had used a soft ball. And we had said nothing about it. Desmond had declared, after a rather ominous pause, that you would never notice it; which was odd, seeing that at the moment we were both standing staring at it. Clearly this was my chance to step forward and set a good example. Instead, instantly I divined what was meant: that if we told, the cricket would be stopped, whereas if we didn't, there was just a chance that the crack might not be discovered—at any rate for some time—since the study was chiefly if not entirely used as a storehouse for books. Deplorably, and without a word spoken, I fell in with this view, and now, just as deplorably, I was tempted to confess to Granny, only it seemed rather late in the day, and I had the feeling that my accomplice would think I had let him down. Not that he really was my accomplice, for ten minutes after the accident I am sure he had forgotten all about it. So I remained guiltily silent, and so far as I ever learned that was the end of the matter.

X

THE BRACKNELS brought me neither fame nor fortune, but it brought me two friendships—with E. M. Forster and with Walter de la Mare—which have lasted from that day till this. E. M. I got to know shortly after the book was published. He had read it, written to me, and a little later, when he was over in Belfast, we met. The spot suggested by him, I find, was the Carlton Restaurant, and I was to recognize him by the clues of "a lightish cloth cap, purple and white scarf, and great coat". I think I should have recognized him without these clues, and I am quite sure that the meeting did not take place in the Carlton, but in my own house, for I have a distinct recollection that Pan and Nyx and Puss were present to welcome him, and that James joined us later. I can even remember James asking him how he thought of his plots—a perfectly natural and innocent question, yet one which no writer would ask, and which rarely elicits responsiveness. De la Mare, out of sheer good nature, would have risen to it determinedly, and the conversation would have become metaphysical. With E. M., who is not metaphysical, the conversation temporarily languished.

"*On goûte à faire des étiquettes une douceur qui se répand dans tout l'être*", and at the time of E. M.'s visit I was mounting my prints of the Old Masters and arranging them according to schools and dates. There is some secret instinct by which collectors instantly recognize one another, and though E. M. was interested in the Old Masters, I divined at once that this interest would not be carried to the point of writing *étiquettes*. Therefore, though surrounding us, and fortunately concealed in boxes, drawers, and cupboards, there were at least half a dozen other collections, I made no allusion to them. To-day I should have no hesitation in mentioning even my collection of stamps. E. M. would not condemn it—condemnation is not in his line. All the same, when he presented me with a special copy of *A Passage to India*, it was accompanied by a note saying he was pandering to the basest of my passions, and, though not seriously, in a sense he meant it, meant that while it was quite harmless, this really was the most one could claim for it. But I had always had a foot firmly planted in the Philistine world: I enjoyed bridge, dog shows, playing in tournaments, book-hunting, print-collecting; and I had even been extremely happy at school, when, like Shelley and everybody else, I ought to have been miserable.

At the date of E. M.'s visit I must have been at work on *Following Darkness*, for when it was finished I dedicated it to him. I cannot remember anything in connection with the origin of this tale except that it was designed as a realistic study of adolescence, and though that to-day will appear a far from original idea, yet it was, I think, the first novel of its kind to be written in English. I am not sure, indeed, that it was not also the last, for *Sinister Street*, which appeared a year later, and all its numerous successors, are certainly in a different tradition, at any rate are placed in a very different world. My world was narrow and provincial on one side, and extending unto the eighth sphere on the other: their's was infinitely more civilized, a world which everybody could recognize and check from memory and observation.

A hint of the supernatural entered into *Following Darkness*, but only because that was inseparable from my conception of reality. And it was perhaps more an atmosphere than anything else. At all events, it included nothing that I was not prepared to vouch for as within my own experience. So far as realism goes, it was on quite other rocks I came to grief—Peter's mother, Katherine's mother, the preparations for a sequel which, if it ever had been written, must have been wildly romantic. These rocks were plainly visible when I came to rewrite the story as *Peter Waring*, and not being indigenous to the theme were easily removed. Even at the time I had been dubious about them, though I had not then seen how to mend matters. Besides, Arnold wanted the book for his Autumn list, so it seemed better to let it go.

The tale was written in the form of an auto-biography, but no circumstances could have been

less like my own than were Peter's. I gave him
some of my early ideas and impressions—those,
namely, that reappear in *Apostate*—but actually I
drew him much more objectively than later I drew
Tom in *Uncle Stephen*. There is only one deliberate
portrait in the book—George—though of course
suggestions for other characters came from real
life—Alice from a little girl in a *pension* at Geneva,
where I had stayed during a long vacation; Aunt
Margaret from the widow of a clergyman, in
whose house I had rooms before going to Cambridge; Gerald from a youth I had met on a
steamer going down the Rhine. Owen, too, had
bits of Andrew in him, and bits of another boy.
But Mrs. Carroll, Katherine, Miss Izzy, Uncle
George, Peter's father—these had no originals
that memory can recapture. And all the incidents
were invented except the incident of the merry-
go-round, which was an altered version of a
scene that had actually taken place when I was
about sixteen.

Following Darkness had a singularly mixed
reception: it seemed either to please greatly or to
offend. It found, for instance, a warm supporter
in Professor Stanley Hall, the American psycholo-
gist, but—— Well, *was* a scientific public what I
chiefly wanted? He wrote to me about the book
at length, and he wrote enthusiastically. "It seems
to me the best presentation of the psychical
phenomena of the adolescent ferment that I have
ever seen. I shall take the liberty, unless you ob-

ject, of referring to it in a forthcoming edition of
my own book on *Adolescence*. I tremendously
wish you, or some one, would write a book on
the same period in girls. I cannot think that Marie
Bashkertseff and others of that ilk are normal."

This pleased me, yet not altogether. If the
truth be told, it caused me at the same time a certain annoyance. It flattered me that I should be
thought capable of writing a similar book about
girls, but the flattery brought me up sharply
against my limitations—limitations of imagination, limitations of sympathy. Sympathy, above
all. In fact the suggestion seemed not very understanding. Quite apart from the question of literary
ability, I could never even attempt to write a
Tess or a *Madame Bovary*—let alone a book about
adolescent girls. I fell back on the question—
Could Hardy have done Stevie in *The Secret
Agent*, or Mr. Jones in *Victory*?

Then came Anne Macdonell's condemnation in
The Manchester Guardian, which was quite as
whole-hearted as Stanley Hall's approval. I had
written a novel, Miss Macdonell declared, that
could only appeal to doctors and to schoolmasters.

Now I myself was at this time reviewing
regularly for *The Manchester Guardian*, and to
attack a colleague is unusual, so I gathered that
her dislike of the book must be strong. I was the
more puzzled, therefore, when in the same paper
she later on devoted a panegyric to *The Spring
Song*, since it seemed to me that despite the varia-

tion in the fable the two stories were quite clearly
from the same hand. Simultaneously she wrote to
me privately saying, "the book delighted me: it
will last, whether or not it has an immediate success". But she repeated her disapproval of *Following Darkness*. "It had some of the features of
Sinister Street, hadn't it? Both seem to waste a good
deal of real talent on what is not very important.
I am willing to face evil, even sordid evil, any
amount of it, in the presentation of the drama of
life, if it is the genuine thing. But a boy's little
experiments in naughtiness, his imitative and
furtive dashes into dark and vicious ways are by
no means always the genuine thing. They are
manifestations of his egoism and not at all
interesting as a rule. Why flatter by elaborate
analysis a boy's silly aping of better sinners than
himself?"

Here, at any rate, were two verdicts, absolutely
contradictory, yet both pronounced by sincere
and intelligent persons. What seemed to Stanley
Hall extremely important, seemed to Miss Macdonell a waste of time. Naturally I agreed with the
former judgement, and still do so. If I had never
written a line, and were never again to write one,
that would not alter my conviction that the years
of childhood, boyhood, and adolescence are the
most significant. What follows is chiefly a logical
development—the child being father of the man.
Most strangely, the only person I have ever found
to agree with me in this is Walter de la Mare, for

we have talked it over many a time. Two seems a
rather small minority, but then most people have
forgotten, lost interest, and their time-conscious-
ness, I think, is less liable to ebb and flow, the
present being much more sharply divided from the
past, with no overlapping, no swaying backward
and forward, no return either in imagination or
dream.

With the general public *Following Darkness*
failed. It was, as I say, either liked a lot, or not at
all, and those who liked it were few. It was, I
thought, the best book I had yet written, and it
was the least successful. The conclusion seemed
obvious—that I was working *away* from popular-
ity, and therefore the closer I approached to
writing the book I wanted to write, the more
unqualified my failure must be. What then was
the use of going on? Once more it was Edmund
Gosse who encouraged me. I wrote to him quite
frankly on the subject, and with equal frankness
he urged me on no account to give up, or to
diverge from the path I had chosen. The contemporary English novel didn't matter; it was
negligible; and in any case I had nothing to do
with it, *Following Darkness* being in the Russian
tradition. Katherine was too remote and starry:
the rest of the book seemed to him real as no novel
he had read for a long time was real. On the other
hand, I presented my incidents too quietly—
without, as it were, sufficient detonation. Where
a Russian would have got a dramatic, even a

startling effect, I kept everything on too low a key. Now I mention Gosse's encouragement the more readily because Max Beerbohm has said that he "was not quick to patronize young men who had done nothing, nor those who had done nothing good. Sidney Colvin would sit demurely benign, exquisitely trustful of the outcome, on any egg—on any number of eggs. Gosse cared but for the fledged and able-bodied chick." Yet I was far from that. I was a chick who in the beginning had strayed from the hennery, and whose subsequent flutterings had been by no means reassuring. Gosse's attitude later on, I confess, seemed to me strange; but then I have always found great difficulty in understanding any one who does not come boldly out into the open— who is discreet, cautious, politic. For example, he never reviewed a book of mine, yet, as I learned later, he actually was asked to make *Apostate* the subject of one of his weekly articles in *The Sunday Times*. He refused, though he had read the book and had written to tell me how much he had enjoyed it, and how often he and Henry James had talked about me and my writings. All this was so unlike what my own attitude would have been in similar circumstances that it perplexed me. Yet he had helped me, had given me confidence when I most needed it, had been extraordinarily kind and sympathetic. And if he did not quite approve, were not his support and sympathy all the more to his credit? I admit that there seems something mildly ironic in the situation, and I should very much like to have overheard one of those conversations he refers to. I don't think they were imaginary. The invention would have been quite gratuitously pointless. But was there, after all these years, a purpose in bringing Henry James in again? I should say possibly, even probably, and if so it can only have been a most gracious one.

XI

I LOVE the sea; yet actually to be *on* the sea very quickly bores me. I love it only from the shore, when I can hear its music. I love a solitary coast and I love it particularly at the end of day. Then the lonely waste of water and the sound of the breaking waves awaken in me a sense of the eternal. I have known those to whom at that hour and in such a place the sea brings a feeling of depression, but to me it brings a kind of peace, not happy, not sad, removing the fret and worry of life, bridging a gulf between two worlds, setting me free from my present imprisonment and drawing me close to a land from which I have been exiled. I cannot analyze, cannot explain this feeling, but it has never changed from the days when I was a young boy. It draws, indeed, a sponge over all the years between, and I am that same boy again, for time has vanished. In the first story I ever wrote—at the age of eleven or twelve—I tried to express this sea spell; I tried again in the very last, *The Retreat*, and the only difference is in the expression; the feeling behind it is unaltered.

I have never believed in any formal religion, but I have experienced an emotion that seemed to me religious. In a chapter in *Apostate* I tried to describe this, but I have been told that I merely described a landscape and a mood, and that the mood had nothing whatever to do with religion. Be this as it may, it was my nearest approach to it, and it was created by some power outside myself. On that blazing summer afternoon above the banks of the Lagan one may say it was created by the stillness of the trees and of the water: on an evening not so long ago, when I was climbing the mountain road to Glenagivney in Donegal, climbing in shadow till suddenly I reached the brow of the hill, one may say it was created by the light into which I abruptly emerged—a glory of sunset glittering on the sea below me and flaming across the sky. On these and similar occasions doubtless the beauty of the natural scene did count for much, but I remember the same feeling coming to me on the Thames embankment just below Savoy Hill and in the crowded lunch hour, when I was simply sitting on a bench watching the movement of a cloud, because I happened to be too early for an appointment I had made. Out of some such attitude towards nature I imagine the religion of primitive man arose. The sound of the leaves, the sound of running water, the richness and beauty of earth and sky and sea, all pointed to the work of divinity, and an anthropomorphic instinct did the rest.

But I have no desire to cling to the words "religion" and "religious" if to anybody the employment of them in such a connection should seem a profanation. It was, let us say then, only a sense that behind the world I was actually gazing upon there existed another world, friendly and benevolent, which I had at one time known, and to which I very much desired to return. This may be a far from rare experience, but at the period I have now reached in my story I had begun to search for some rational justification for such irrational glimpses and intuitions—some explanation of them that might be intellectually acceptable. There seemed clearly only one person to be consulted—and that person was A. E.

So I wrote to him, and at the same time, thinking it might prepare the ground, sent him a copy of *Following Darkness*. I did not explain my purpose, but I did say that I should like to call when there would be no other visitors present. He replied that he should be quite alone on the two days after Christmas, so on Saint Stephen's day I travelled up to Dublin, and took a room for the night in a dingy hotel in Harcourt Street.

That I should have had such an idea does not seem to me strange, for I had heard much of A. E. from Colum and others, though I had never met him. I was, indeed, going with something of the same purpose as induced Peter to go to the clergyman in *Peter Waring*, and, full of this purpose, it did not even occur to me that A. E. might suppose an admiration for his poetry or pictures to have anything to do with the matter. In point of fact I *had* no great admiration for them. As an artist, I thought he repeated himself, and that his talent, though genuine, was very slight. I went because from what I had been told I imagined, or hoped, that he had found the "way", possessed the secret of life; and indeed this was true so far as he himself was concerned. But the secret of life, I am now persuaded, is not one that can be shared except with those born under the same star and of the same habit of mind.

In those days I was more optimistic and more receptive. I had lunch at my hotel and then set out, wondering what might come of the interview. The house, when I reached it, I found to be a small house in a rather scrubby-looking street, and A. E. himself came to the door in answer to my knock. I saw a big stout man, with a brown beard, brown rough hair scattered over a low narrow forehead, and brown, rather small eyes, gleaming benignly behind spectacles. His face had character and strength, but was not markedly intellectual; it was the face of an artist, I immediately thought, not that of a philosopher, and it was the philosopher I had come to see. On the other hand, a natural kindliness and benevolence radiated from him, his clumsy movements reminded me of those of a large and friendly dog, I felt instantly at home and at my ease. A. E. might not be so great a man as Yeats, but he was an infinitely more approachable one.

He brought me into a room, the walls of which were covered with pictures, mostly his own. There were pictures even on the floor, and he told me that in the last ten years he had painted about seven hundred. We sat down and began to talk.

His first words were disconcerting. "You're a realist," A. E. said, and smiled.

Now Edmund Gosse had told me that I was a realist and I had been pleased; so why should A. E.'s words not have pleased me? I don't know, except that for some reason I fancied "realism", for him, meant his friend George Moore, and though I had published an essay on George Moore in the *Westminster Review*, he was not, and never could be, one of my writers. At all events, I had not come to discuss realism—or any literary question. I had my own views on these subjects and was pretty sure they were unlikely to be A. E.'s. Yet for a long time we continued to talk of books, arriving nowhere, for on no single point were we in agreement. A.E. took down volumes from the shelves and read passages aloud, and quoted passages. I listened, and decided that what he was chiefly interested in was the raw material of literature. Presently I mentioned some of my own favourite writers, but they were not his, and I even felt that he knew very little about them, certainly not enough to dismiss them as easily as he did. Anatole France he dismissed in a sentence, and I discovered—rather tactlessly perhaps, since it was by direct questioning—that he had read only one or two of his books, and those in an English translation. He said that Conrad had a wooden style and had never written a beautiful line: he said that *The Turn of the Screw* merely showed that Henry James knew nothing about ghosts: he said that Keats, Shelley, Coleridge, and Yeats were all second-rate poets, because their work had not its origin in the whole life of man, but only in particular aspects of life and in individual moods, whereas Walt Whitman was a first-rate poet. Of Edgar Poe he spoke slightingly, and Arthur Symons he described as a dilettante in criticism, who had written about Symbolism merely because he thought it was the proper thing to do.

Before long I found myself contradicting these views rather freely, and I got the impression that A. E. was not accustomed to contradiction. He took it quite good-naturedly, however; certainly not in the least as Doctor Johnson would have done. The novelists he admired were Kipling and Dumas. There seemed to be an inconsistency here, for if Conrad had failed because he had never written a beautiful line, why was not the same criticism applicable to Kipling and Dumas? In my opinion Conrad had written many beautiful lines, but the criterion by which A. E. judged a novelist was to ask himself whether or not in olden times that novelist would have been a teller of tales seated at the gate of Bagdad. Kipling and Dumas would; Conrad and Henry James would not.

I somehow imagined that he had said this before: in fact, that he had been over all the ground

many times, which gave him the advantage a
skilled debater has over a neophyte. By now, too,
I was pretty sure that I did not belong to the
school of Bagdad—hence his first remark, and my
instinctive reaction to it, which I had not understood at the time. But sweeping generalizations
rarely persuade me, though I may make them
myself. Why should not Conrad's Marlowe have
spun his yarns at the gate of Bagdad if he could
spin them on board a ship? It seemed to me, indeed, that the phrase was more picturesque than
critical. One thing was certain, we were not pro-
gressing in the right direction.

A. E. began to talk about Yeats, and of an
enthusiastic essay I had written about his early
work. He mentioned certain poems that Yeats
had spoiled, and expressed the view that, so far as
actual writing goes, hasty work is the best. Yet a
little later he poured scorn on the idea of novelists
such as Arnold Bennett and Henry James, who
wrote as much in a year as Milton did in a lifetime, hoping to contribute anything to literature.
He told me Yeats was suffering from a hereditary
disease which made it impossible for him not to
tinker with things. His father, the painter, was
the same, and ruined all his portraits by working
over them till the canvas was a mere load of paint.
He told me a lot of amusing stories about Yeats,
but there was nothing malicious in them, and he
did full justice to the beauty of Yeats's verse,
which he said had in it a quality of music that

made any other poet despair, that indeed had rarely been equalled and never surpassed.

Here at last we were in complete agreement, and yet I was not sure that my enthusiasm wholly pleased him. Of course to-day I can see that there was something else, and can see that this was perfectly natural. A. E. was a sage, but he was, too, an artist, and the artist is a very sensitive person. If it was to Yeats I gave my whole admiration, why hadn't I gone to see Yeats, why had I come to see him? But the sage triumphed, and the tactlessness I now recognize as mine. In spite of it, in spite of differences of opinion, it was all very pleasant and perfectly friendly. I liked A. E.; I liked the little boy to whom he introduced me; and I liked the big shaggy dog whose name I have forgotten.

All the same, this was not what I had come for, nor was it till a meal had intervened that I succeeded in turning the conversation away from literature and in approaching the true object of my visit. That again was my fault, for how could he have guessed what I wanted? True, I had hoped he might from *Following Darkness*, but *Following Darkness* evidently had impressed him only as an experiment in naturalism.

I have no recollection how, or by what gradations, we got on to the desired ground, but I know that as the evening wore on A. E. began to talk of his psychical experiences. Here without qualification I was prepared to play the part of

Boswell, contributing nothing except attentive-
ness and an occasional question. It was, I discovered, much the best method with A. E. He
told me that he had seen as plainly as he now saw
me, beings who were not of this world. When the
little boy I have mentioned had been a baby, he
had seen these unearthly beings watching over
him while he lay asleep. I knew he was perfectly
sincere, but I knew my own experiences, and I
knew also, by this time, that my mind was much
more sceptical than A. E.'s. I mentioned the
difficulty of getting a positive proof. I don't
suppose he found me particularly receptive, but
I was at least not a materialist and was very much
interested; and presently, for these reasons, he
began to instruct me in the "way".

First, one must learn to concentrate, and he
explained how one should set about this. It was a
matter of practice, and I may say here that I
actually did practise it for several days, though
the performance was neither easy nor entertaining;
what A. E. had suggested that I should concentrate upon being an imaginary triangle. Next, one
must learn to meditate, and the method of this
also was explained—*my* kind of wool-gathering
meditation being quite useless. On the other hand,
if I followed A. E.'s instructions, at the end of
two months I should find my life in a turmoil,
while at the end of six I should find myself looking back on my present state as to-day I looked
back on my childhood.

In the Greeks and in Greek religion A. E. did not seem much interested: he had discovered his own teachers in the East. But when he spoke of the unity of all religions I felt we were drawing closer to what I sought. Unfortunately it was also becoming ever clearer to me that the Eastern mysticism of A. E. was as alien from my way of thinking and feeling as was Christianity. In fact, it produced upon me much the same effect. It did not attract me; I did not really like it; I was outside the pale.

A. E. had begun to tell me of the use of symbols. He had met Gerald Balfour, the president of the Society for Psychical Research, and had asked him why they went about their investigations in so wrong a way: why they ignored so completely the way of the mystics: why they had never even experimented with symbols? Gerald Balfour, however, knew nothing about symbols, and said so. A. E. explained how the word Egypt, to take a very simple example, inevitably and instantaneously calls up a vision of pyramids and sphinxes, and how by employing certain symbols to be found in the Sacred Books one can, by the same law of association, call up in the vaster memory of nature particular visions. They agreed to experiment through the post, and to prevent any danger of telepathy A. E. sent Gerald Balfour a symbol which he was sure nobody in England would know. He painted it on the outside of an envelope, and inside he put the explanation.

Gerald Balfour wrote to tell him that he had given the unopened envelope to a medium, who had held it against her forehead. After a time she said that she could get nothing except an impression of water, but that she was very tired and it was all vague.

The next day they tried again, and this time the impression of water became more definite. It was a well, or a pond, and the water was of a purplish colour. Over the pond hazel-trees were hanging, and there seemed to be some kind of reddish fruit dropping down from them on to the surface. That was all. But the symbol was the symbol of Manannan macLir and the Nuts of Knowledge. The Nuts of Knowledge grew on a hazel-tree, and macLir was the controller of the waters.

I wondered if Yeats had learned about Symbolism from A. E., or if A. E. had learned from Yeats, or if they had arrived at their beliefs independently, but I asked no question. If one indeed initiated the other, I am inclined to think the initiator was A. E.

It was late when I left the house: indeed I must have paid an unconscionably long visit, for I had arrived early in the afternoon and it was now one o'clock in the morning. The night was frosty and there was a moon. I had a long walk from Rathgar Avenue to Harcourt Street, but A. E. set me on my way, and I enjoyed it: the streets were silent and deserted, the houses dark, and the air clear and cold.

This was our first meeting. Later I saw him frequently—every time I went to Dublin—and I wrote for his paper, *The Irish Statesman*, so long as it existed. He was the kindest of men, and I never met another Irishman in whom the qualities of North and South were so perfectly balanced. He was in himself the symbol of a United Ireland. He had the gift of bringing people together, of reconciling opposites, of pouring oil on troubled waters. And the waters in Ireland are always troubled—if it isn't politics it is religion. As a race we are like that—though I myself was never sufficiently public-spirited to be embroiled. But think of the rows over the *Playboy*, even over *The Countess Cathleen!* And even I, in my innocence, once nearly exploded a mine. The unsuspected spark was an article called *Bishops and Black Magic*—really a review of Richard Garnett's *The Twilight of the Gods*—but by return of post I received a letter from A. E.

My dear Forrest Reid,

You do not know that I have at present four or five clerical papers subjecting everything which appears in *The Irish Statesman* to a microscopic investigation, and your article on *Bishops and Black Magic* would give them the joy of their lives. I like it very much, it pleased me and amused me, but I wonder whether you could find some other quotation than that delightful one with the dialogue between the sorcerer and the bishop? And

in the name of God find another title! When my
review of Stephen McKenna's *Plotinus* led to a
vehement article in a clerical journal—saying that
I was a pagan and inculcating paganism—you can
guess what your article associating bishops with
Black Magic would lead to; though I am inclined
to think that to be a bishop of any religion is to
operate in the Black Art!

Yours ever,

A. E.

On turning over a bundle of A. E.'s letters in
search of the one just quoted I came upon another,
recording an incident which I had completely
forgotten. Actually the conversation referred to
was never repeated to me; the first I heard of the
matter was this, his own denial of it, which is so
characteristic that I give it in full.

7th May, 1924.

My dear Forrest Reid,

It has been repeated to me that some person who came to my house retailed to you some
conversation with regard to you or your work in
which I was represented as slighting it. I wish to
say that if this was retailed to you it is an absolute
fabrication or else a statement by somebody so
foolish and unintelligent that he was incapable of
understanding what was said. I always speak my
mind with perfect frankness about literature and
if I thought your writing not good I would say
so to you as frankly as I would say it to anybody

else. What I wrote to you about your memories of childhood represented what I thought and I would not say to others anything else. I thought the essay delightful, I thought it the best *writing* of yours I have ever seen, though you always write with distinction. I have praised sincerely your novels whenever I have spoken about them, and indeed the only criticism I ever remember making about your work was in regard to some praise you gave to a poem of Yeats which I did not think one of his best. I think you quoted "Bow down, archangels, in your dim abode", and the lines that followed as more beautiful than Milton. I am not sure that I did not speak to you yourself upon this. My objection to the verse was that I could not know what was meant by

"Weary and kind one lingered by His seat".

If this referred to the Eternal Beauty the adjectives "weary and kind" are meaningless. If they referred to the woman they are equally meaningless, because it suggests that the Almighty had before the beginning of the world imagined this woman of to-day as "weary and kind". That was my reason for thinking the verse had no fundamental brainwork and was not good Yeats or profound poetry. And this criticism is the only criticism I ever made of your work, and if any person says otherwise he is a conscious liar or an unconscious fool unable to gather in the meaning of words. I write to you because I respect your talent and like yourself, and would be sorry if any false report, in this country of idle tongues, should make you think otherwise.

Yours sincerely,
GEORGE RUSSELL.

Here are the lines:

> Bow down, archangels, in your dim abode:
> Before you were, or any hearts to beat,
> Weary and kind one lingered by His seat;
> He made the world to be a grassy road
> Before her wandering feet.

But A. E. is not quite right. I did not say that the lines were more beautiful than anything in Milton; I am inclined to be careful about such statements, and all I said was that they recalled Milton. The actual passage will be found on page 86 of my book on Yeats:

"Sometimes a poem opens out slowly, with a sort of spreading, increasing movement that breaks at last into a proud lonely magnificence of phrasing, as in the concluding lines of *The Rose of the World*." Then I give the lines quoted above, and add: "Here, no doubt, much depends upon the solemn grandeur of a single phrase, which recalls the splendour of Milton's

> Where the bright Seraphim in burning row. . . .

Well, what I said then, in 1915, I should repeat to-day, a quarter of a century later. It is perfectly plain that I was talking of Yeats's poetic style, and it must be perfectly plain, for anybody who has an ear, that I was not talking foolishly. But all depends on that. Nor should I call the poem obscure. The obscurity of modern verse, which has little or no music, seems to me deplorable, but here, through the music, I am brought directly into touch with the poet's mind, and without any tedious process of translation, which the wise artist never imposes.

But A. E. was perfectly correct about the "country of idle tongues", though in this connection I should call them spiteful and evil tongues. I know of one case in which I myself was reported to have said something that I never said and never thought, the deliberate intention being to make mischief. Moreover it succeeded, because unfortunately, not having met the persons concerned, unlike A. E., I took no active and immediate steps to kill the lie.

The origin of such falsehoods is invariably—whether inspired by jealousy or not—a desire to wound, odious and cowardly as that of the writer of anonymous letters. It is quite conceivable that the liar in both cases was the same person, and I hope so. I hope there were not two of them. At any rate, I assured A. E. that I had heard nothing, and he replied:

My dear F. R.

I am glad to hear from your letter that the conversation reported to me was a pure invention. I have suffered so much from opinions attributed to me by unintelligent people or those who are consciously malicious that I always like to make clear to those I respect and like what I really do think. I enquired further into the origin of the report and showed your letter to the person who reported to me the rumour, and he is now hunting out the originator of the rumour, who is, I understand, in Dublin at present, and was not in Belfast at all for some time. I hope to have a further explanation through this channel as to what excuse the originator of the rumour offers. I think it is always a good thing to expose a social liar.

Yours sincerely,

A. E.

Whether he succeeded in exposing this particular social liar or not I never learned, and am rather vexed now that I didn't take more interest in the matter. A. E. withholds names, but I expect he would have told me if I had asked him to, unless sworn to secrecy. Clearly there was an enemy lurking in the shadow, but on the evidence it is difficult to decide whether he was mine or A. E.'s, or indeed to discover any purpose in his action.

And I cannot imagine anybody being A. E.'s enemy. He was himself so kind, so straight-forward, so genuine. It was typical of him that when his son wanted to visit Belfast he should send him to me without any preliminary fuss, merely with a note to say that he had been sent to stay for a week-end with me if I would have him. That is the kind of thing I like, the kind of relation I value. In such matters at least we were at one, even if in the matter of religion I found it harder to follow him. For the return to, the reabsorption into, the divine mind, seemed to me terribly like extinction. It does so still. Take a very homely illustration. This lettuce I have just been munching is (I trust!) being absorbed into a higher form of life, but as a lettuce what does it gain from that? What of those garden days when the dark soil was soft beneath it, when the dew fell on its young green leaves, and the sunshine and the rain? A pagan I went to A. E., and a pagan, I am afraid, at heart and in spirit, I bade farewell to him.

On the following day I returned home. My railway carriage was divided into compartments, and from the next compartment a small boy was gazing at me with dark bright eyes that had in them a kind of gentleness, like the gentleness of an animal. He was with his mother and two younger sisters. Presently he knelt up on the seat and leaned over my shoulder, and I heard a soft voice say in my ear, "John Silence". It was the name of the book I had bought to read in the train. He began to play little tricks and very soon climbed over the back of the seat and sat beside me. He showed me the book *he* had—an odd volume of *London Society*, dating back to the 'Sixties. I asked him what kind of books he liked, and gave him to

read the chapter in *John Silence* describing the
laying of the ghost. He understood it, though it
was written in a psychological jargon, and when
he had finished he asked me how much the book
cost. So I gave him my copy and at once he became absorbed in it as if he had fallen into a
dream. I asked his mother how old he was. He
was eight, and had read *Pilgrim's Progress* when he
was six. He had read Dickens and Ballantyne and
everything he could lay his hands on, but she
would not let him join a library because this
would interfere with his lessons and his music.
They lived in Portadown, and I imagined them
to be of the small-shopkeeping class.

And suddenly I realized that all this was
obliterating the lessons I had learned from A. E.
The human touch, the human interest—these had
but to show themselves for a moment, and the
doctrines of contemplation and detachment faded
out. Except that I had made friends with A. E.,
I might as well have stayed at home.

XII

Three toy boats sailing on a pond;
    A stone god watching, frozen, through the trees;
    Dead leaves that dance around his pedestal;
Pale clouds and winter sun beyond.

A tune, a melody that floats,
    Whispers and whistles through the naked trees;
    A fountain rising, falling; faded skies;
The moving whiteness of the children's boats.

SO I described it on the spot, for at this time I still kept up a habit, begun in my schooldays, of carrying a note-book in which I jotted down impressions—impressions of places or pictures or people—rarely or never thoughts. They were thumb-nail sketches, memoranda that might or might not be used later, and this one was used, and slightly expanded as I turned it into prose and fitted it into its place.

"Allingham recrossed the river and strolled back to the gardens of the Tuileries, that were grey and delicate in the gathering dusk. He continued his walk on through the Bois de Boulogne. There, beside a pond on which some children were sailing toy boats, he came to a standstill. Through the trees a stone god watched, frozen, silent. Brown dead leaves twirled about his pedestal, and a humming of wind passed overhead, like the murmur of an Aeolian harp. In the middle of the pond a fountain rose against the darkening sky. A faint white light seemed to drop down upon the whiteness of the children's boats. The scene had a remote, ghostly quality: it was as if he had imagined it, and by merely turning away his thoughts could draw a veil over it again: and all the time a wind music passed and repassed in thin arpeggios among the rustling leaves. . . .

"The children played liked dream children, and in Allingham's mind the whole picture took on a strangely poetic quality, a quality as of something re-enacted in the spirit, that had happened long ago. His mind was filled with memories. They hovered before him, and their soft wings brushed his face, like the wings of moths."

There you have a passage from my next novel, *The Gentle Lover*, and the passage is more or less typical of the entire book, or at least of what I intended it to be.

The Gentle Lover was to furnish a complete contrast to *Following Darkness*; it was to be light and gay and to contain nothing that the eye and the mind could not dwell upon with pleasure. But as usual the achievement fell far below the conception. As later, in *The Spring Song*, I made the mistake of introducing a melodramatic figure, though in *The Spring Song* there was a good deal more excuse for him, since he was an essential part of the story. Here he was not essential. But, wandering about the dark silent streets of Bruges

at night, I could not help imagining some such
person. And then the story, I felt, was just a little
thin, needed an incident or two. To a realist it is a
severe handicap to be by temperament romantic,
unless, like Flaubert, he is sufficiently resolute to
keep the two elements in his nature separate, and
write alternate books in which, without confusing,
he expresses both of them. I think I found the
way eventually, but for a long time, and certainly
in *The Gentle Lover*, I fumbled.

This work had for sub-title, a Comedy of
Middle Age, and I dare say it answers well enough
to that description if the word "comedy" be
taken in the French sense of it. That at least was
what I intended. The primary title was chosen by
James Rutherford, and I never liked it, even felt
a certain reluctance to pronounce the words,
which seemed to me not at all in my line. But from
a practical point of view James was right: the
book, on the strength of its title, sold better than
either *The Bracknels* or *Following Darkness*, though
it was inferior to both.

I am by no means indifferent to titles, and I
believe I know when I have got the right one.
Once or twice I have failed badly, but I knew I
had failed. *The Kingdom of Twilight* was bad. That
is hardly surprising, for it was bad in exactly the
same way as everything else in the book was bad.
At the Door of the Gate was bad, and less excusably,
for I at least have an ear, and the verse jingle is
obvious. Even the kind of verse—Austin Dob-

son's. It would go, I should think, something like this:

> At the door of the gate
>   I had waited some time;
> I was sure she was late
> At the door of the gate,
> For a clock had struck eight,
>   I had just heard it chime.
> At the door of the gate
>   I had waited some time.

Is it really either much better or much worse than Dobson's

> These are leaves of my rose,
>   Pink petals I treasure:
> There is more than one knows
> In the leaves of my rose;
> O, the joys, O the woes!——
>   They are quite beyond measure.
> These are leaves of my rose,
>   Pink petals I treasure.

The Gentle Lover was the direct result of loiterings in Bruges and Italy. Its subject was a Henry James subject—one of those *amours de voyage* that Henry in his youth was so fond of treating. But he treated them with an urbanity, a distinction, a sustained lightness of touch and beauty of texture that were quite beyond me, and indeed have never been approached by any other novelist. Besides, the subject was definitely not mine. Of course I am looking at it now across a wide gulf of years. At the time, I dare say, I felt very differently. Except under compulsion I could not now sit down to write *The Gentle Lover*, or *At the Door of the Gate*, or even *Pender*. I could not feel sufficient interest in them. My last attempt to write an ordinary novel for ordinary readers was when, on finishing *Pender*, I mapped out a full-length tale based on the famous trial of Madeleine Smith. I called it *Nina Westby* (the surname I used later in a book of a very different nature). The arrangement of the plot interested me while I *was* arranging it: in fact it was full of what are called "strong situations", and all went well until I invented a younger brother for Nina. He was a boy of seventeen, and I sketched a scene in which he is working late in his own room for a scholarship examination, when Nina suddenly interrupts him. He looks up, rather white and tired, with ruffled hair and very young, innocent eyes. Anybody but Nina would have spared him. She, however, is not of the sparing sort, besides being at her wits' end to find somebody to help her. She knows her brother is affectionate and loyal; she must get back the incriminating letters she has written to her lover; so she forces her highly disagreeable confidences upon him, and at the same time effectually dished my book. The brother, you see, like Justin in *Madame Bovary*, was designed to supply the glimpse of moral beauty that Nina's history most certainly required if it was not to be an unrelieved chronicle of the base and the sordid. And he did this, but with the immediate effect that he became the centre of the story. Poor Nina could not survive that contact for a moment. The tragedy became his not hers, and I saw I should never write my novel, or if I did, that it would not be the novel I had planned.

To return to *The Gentle Lover*; I dedicated it when it was finished to John McBurney, and it was characteristic of him that he only told me this had pleased him when he was on his death-bed. Yet at the time the book was written he was one of my closest friends.

Our first meeting had been in a public-house, the Globe. I have forgotten who introduced us— but probably, since it was a pub, either Parkhill or Reynolds. At any rate, I took a dislike to him because he told me an indecent story—a thing I detest. Long afterwards, when we were intimate friends, I mentioned this, whereupon he immediately told me another—but that was to be expected.

In the beginning, too, I think I was slightly repelled physically, for he was a consumptive. These things either matter to one or they don't: and when they do, it is no use pretending that they don't. To me they do; yet the odd thing is that no animal, even if afflicted with the most repulsive disease, repels me. I hasten to add that whatever this first reaction may have been, it did not last, could not have lasted; we became friends.

McBurney was a man of extraordinary courage and personal charm. Of all those I have ever met I think he had the nimblest wit and the most generous nature. He was certainly very lovable, though this quality was not revealed to everybody. On occasion, in fact, he could be exactly the opposite. His father had been a working man who was always out of work; he himself had received the rudiments of an education at a National School, and had run about the streets barefoot. He was put to serve his apprenticeship as a damask designer in a firm that kept no designer to teach him. But he attended night classes at the School of Art and won a scholarship to South Kensington. When he returned to Belfast he got a good position as a designer, but an attack of hæmorrhage put an end to that, and for six months he was in hospital.

When I got to know him he was working on his own account—was what in journalism would be called a "free lance"—making for linen manufacturers designs of "kittens catching butterflies", or "butterflies catching kittens"—it really didn't much matter which, for he had no illusions about them. He was a small man, very dark, with dark bright eyes, a trimmed black beard, and a pale face. His nature was comprised of a curious blend of melancholy and gaiety, with an underlying pride that nothing could shake. His health was wretched and he took no care of himself, yet right up to the end the spirit was alert, whimsical, witty as ever, in the frail exhausted body. His early ambition of becoming a painter had been abandoned. For one thing, he had not the necessary physical strength. He himself knew precisely the

value of the landscapes and portraits he less and
less frequently produced: he had no vanity, no
jealousy of others, and a very beautiful intelligence. The whole thing was tragic, for from the
beginning he had had no chance, yet he was of
the salt of the earth. I used to call at his office
and sit watching him designing kittens catching
butterflies, for it was a labour that permitted a free
flow of conversation. I played billiards with him,
and met him also at the Arts Club. I was very
much attached to him. On that last winter, when
he was dying, I used to sit with him in an ice-cold
bedroom, for he was not allowed a fire, and the
window was kept as wide open as it would go.
And though I wrapped myself up in overcoats or
rugs there were afternoons when I came away half
frozen. It was at this time—when he could do
nothing else—that he began his novel. This work
I knew, of course, was designed primarily for my
benefit, and I don't believe he ever touched it
except when he was expecting me, or when I was
leaving. Then he would ask me to give it to him.
I never saw it—I never saw more than the large
thick black notebook I placed in his hands, and
in which, he declared, it was being written. I
don't know whether he ever really did write anything. If he did, it was certainly a burlesque, but
I imagine it was only a pretence invented to tease
me: one writes a novel when one is past doing
anything else. It was horribly pathetic, and I had
to struggle to maintain a light and careless tone,

for he loathed any overt display of emotion. In those last weeks I came very close to him, but we never mentioned what was going to happen, though we both knew it was approaching steadily and rapidly. For him it would be the end of all things; for me the end of a friendship that had been unlike any other. There was no repining, no depression. When I think of the Christian terror and gloom that beset Doctor Johnson at the thought of death, I cannot help feeling that there is much to be said for paganism.

Also, though it may have hastened his death, I think McBurney was right to lead his own life until the end. By care he might have prolonged it, but he agreed with the great Doctor that only a scoundrel thinks of going to bed before twelve o'clock. He had been all his life a noctambulist in his habits, and nothing could cure him of it. Ten o'clock or later was for him the normal time to begin an evening. He would then want to play billiards, and after that sit talking in the smoking room of the Arts Club until the small hours, when we would sally forth in search of Johnston's donkey-cart, which was usually to be found at the corner of Chichester Street. From Johnston you could obtain chips and fried fish and poloneys, served in pieces of newspaper. You ate these delicacies in your fingers, for Johnston knew nothing of knives and forks and plates, and you ate them standing there in the street. Johnston's cart was a rallying spot for late spirits—mostly youthful toughs. McBurney's appearance—probably owing to that black pointed beard—occasionally aroused comment. "Christ! a bloody Jew eating chips!"—that kind of thing. Believe it or not—and he would never believe it—the remark would be made without the least intention of offensiveness. Probably because I felt more friendly towards them, I was invariably treated by the toughs as one of themselves, or at any rate as an approachable person. McBurney, I don't know why, seemed to regard this approachableness with disfavour. We would stand in a ring round the cart, eating our greasy fish and chips—I could never quite stomach a poloney, though I have no doubt they were excellent—while the patient donkey dozed and I scratched him under his venerable ears. Johnston himself was converted, and occasionally objected to the conversation, without, I must say, much effect. The language *was* at times pretty awful, only, as the speakers did not realize this, and were quite well-intentioned, nobody ever knew what would offend Johnston and what would not. They didn't wish to offend him, but they had no other vocabulary, and the expletives were as mechanical and meaningless as parrot cries. To my surprise, the most vehement objection Johnston ever made was to a remark of my own. I have forgotten what it was, but, considering the ordinary talk of his customers, it must have been the content rather than the expression that he disapproved of, since at no time have I been addicted to bad language. With the converted, however, you never can tell, and Johnston was a member of the Salvation Army, though he did not wear a uniform when plying his trade.

Gradually the party would break up, and we would pursue our several ways homeward. McBurney lived up the Antrim Road, I in the opposite direction. And in the summer, crossing Ormeau Bridge, dawn would be breaking, the trees in the park would be already green, the birds beginning to twitter.

He was as loyal a friend as I have ever had, and I think of him more, have missed him more perhaps, than any other. More even than Andrew, because our friendship never suffered change or diminution. *Requiescat in pace!*

At the beginning of this chapter I alluded to a notebook I kept. For the sake of completeness I here give a few samples of the kind of notes it contained.

As a rule there is no more than an attempt to crystallize an impression. Thus:

"Drumbo.

"Big dark branches seen through the yellow chestnut leaves. A twisting path, brown with a carpet of fallen leaves. An avenue leading to an unseen house. Green fields on either side, drifted over with leaves. And the grey stone posts of the gate. A solitary black horse and one or two cows. Yellow, green, and dark bronze turning to black. An open iron gate."

It is clear that this, if I ever wished to bring Drumbo into a story, would be more suggestive than a snapshot taken with a camera could be.

Slightly different, because less baldly impressionistic, is the following:

"I know not why the sight of an old brown horse plodding slowly down the road by himself should move me to the very depths of tenderness and affection. He enters a field where a donkey is grazing. The donkey looks up and they recognize each other. It all seems a part of the autumn spirit, and a link, though I cannot explain why or how, between the present and the past. The horse and donkey are really old acquaintances, I imagine, but animals have a way of making and receiving communications that we must have lost. I myself have established relations with a butterfly by merely wishing to, so that actually he alighted on my outstretched hand—a Red Admiral—and I have done the same with a starling who had flown down my chimney by mistake, and with wasps and with bees."

Now and then, when I was beginning to write, I would elaborate such notes, though simply for my own amusement. The three following must have been written while I was still in the tea trade, and though essentially of a similar kind, obviously have been licked into shape. The first is of a picture, *The Old Barge*, by Edward Stott.

"Twilight: the last flush of evening: the still water of the canal. . . . A white horse drawing a barge: three naked boys upon the river bank: the figures of the bargeman, his wife, and two children. . . . A sky of faint greens and yellows: sunset—subdued, waning, lighting for a moment with dull gold the surface of the water, and touching the horse's back, the flesh of the bathers.

"The boys have turned to watch the horse. Two of them are sitting and one is standing. And they, and the horse, and the other figures, and the landscape, all form a part of the evening quiet. . . .

"The peacefulness, the peculiar solitude and hush of twilight, give a note of poetry to the picture, which seems to fade as you watch it, to grow darker as the night creeps down over the hills.

"Just as in nature, so too here, all is changing, growing clearer, again fading, the figures themselves seeming to live and to move. Gradually while I watch it the whole thing draws closer, gathers about me; the boys are boys I have always known, with whom I played in my own boyhood; the river is a river in which I have bathed—the Lagan. The faint winds whisper as they pass; the evening is filled with the endless murmur of summer. The thing is here and now; it is about me as

I write; I can smell the grass, and feel the cool wind, and hear the ripple of the water as the barge moves through it. Only that horse plodding along the path will never reach the bathers; those boys will never plunge into the river; the night that is so near will never quite descend.

"Move a little to the right and the horse approaches you, the bargeman seated at the helm turns his head, the light seems to lift for a moment, the boys to look almost into your face. And the beauty of the thing grows clearer and clearer, broader and broader, like a flame fanned by the wind."

I was always writing such impressions of pictures. I used to stand before them in galleries until I was half hypnotized, and sometimes, I confess, began to see what wasn't there. Then I would take out my notebook and begin to write.

Here is a note on Westminster Abbey—I suppose about as hackneyed a subject as I could have chosen, but I was very young and it was my first visit to England.

"In this London June there is no coolness to be found except in Westminster Abbey, and for an hour or so I have been wandering about its aisles and chapels. What as much as anything else gives me the spirit of the place, its extraordinary power to draw the present back into the past, is the name, here and there, of a choir-boy, carved in the oak seat he had used two hundred, three hundred years ago. These names will live

as long as those on the marble tombs, longer than
those on the slabs upon the floor, most of which
are already worn away by the trampling of in-
numerable feet. And after all, they tell much the
same story. To me they tell more, for though their
owners have long since mouldered into dust, and
that dust certainly does not lie here, the ghostly
part of them is present, and the music of their
voices still floats faintly on the cool dim air. At
least, I seemed to hear it when, in the late afternoon,
I watched the sun pouring through a side window.
Then also it was that I got the full impression of
the solemnity and majesty which rests over all.

"Westminster School is close at hand, and while
I sat in the cloisters a troop of noisy schoolboys
suddenly entered, on their way to Dean's Yard.
In an instant the entire scene changed, became
full of life and animation. Far more than the sunshine on the square plot of grass, these boys
brought out the age of the Abbey, its grey
crumbling walls and mouldering carvings: and
when they were passed on their way, the silence
that ensued seemed doubly impressive for its
added quality of loneliness, of a sudden and
inexplicable loneliness."

I cannot help finding something rather pathetic
in this note, for it was written, as I say, on my
first visit to London, when I myself was a boy;
and yet, reading it, one would think I was as old
as the "eagle cock that blinks and blinks on

Ballygawley Hill". I didn't know a soul of course, and for a fortnight almost the only words I exchanged were with the head waiter of the hotel and an occasional policeman. My first visit to Paris was very similar, and how I can have enjoyed these excursions is now a mystery. In Paris my entire time was spent in the Louvre, the Luxembourg, the Jardin des Plantes, or in book-hunting along the banks of the Seine; though I did make a vain attempt to discover the Théatre des Marionettes, because Anatole France had written about it. I packed the books I bought in an empty sugar case—Tate's, as I recollect—the bottom of which came out at the railway station, with the result that I very nearly missed my train. But that was on my way home. In Paris I lived in the Rue Saint Honoré; I went to bed early and got up early. In the evenings I sometimes sat at a table in an open-air café, and that was my sole experience of the night-life. If there were temptations to anything more lurid, I was unconscious of them. My mind was filled with books and pictures, and in spite of my youth, or perhaps because of it, nobody tried to lure me from the path of virtue. I don't think I was bored—it was all so strange to me—but certainly I should have liked a companion.

Here is the last note I shall inflict:

"From time to time the snow falls from the roof with a dull heavy thud. It is thawing fast. When I look out into the night a desolate picture is spread before me under the bright moon. It is like something of Edgar Poe's; and with a volume of his tales for company, I turn back to the fire.

"He was a man 'whom Sorrow named his friend'. His art is sad, inhuman, fearful. In it there is little of this earth, nothing of ordinary life. The world that is called up is some dark nameless planet swimming in a black, remote sky.

"Yet these tales and poems are beautiful in their fashion—the poems above all. But the beings who move in them are visions, phantoms, dream-things without flesh and blood, misty forms, creatures of another world than ours, creatures of some dim fantastic land which touches ours only in sleep or in the languor following on some long sickness or fever of the body—and perhaps in death. Their beauty is dark, strange, and haunted —a beauty into which all the grim secrets of the grave have passed. Ulalume, The Sleeper, Leonore—they have raised the veil of mortality and gazed into 'the distant Aidenn'.

"A low murmur rising swiftly to a long shrill cry passes just above the house and dies slowly in the distance. It is the wind coming from I know not whence and passing I know not whither, but for a moment it seemed something more ghostly, a cry from the other side."

If I had been a writer of verse I probably should have put such fancies into verse, but it was only very rarely that I did so. I wrote them in prose, and of course there is no objection to that if one avoids preciosity. I am afraid I didn't. Let me confess it: I have even tinkered with what you have just been reading—removing adornments. In those days I should have added to them, now I eliminate them, but is not the impulse much the same: can the Ethiopian change his skin or the leopard his spots?

XIII

"I CAN remember a winter afternoon many years ago, when in the University Library at Cambridge I was prowling round the shelves upstairs and took down by the merest chance a thin pale-blue volume called *Songs of Childhood*, by Walter Ramal. I had never heard of Walter Ramal, and the book opened at *The Silver Penny*. . . . It was as if in the silence and fading light of that deserted library I had, like some adventurer in the Middle Ages, sailed all unexpectedly into sight of an unknown and lovely shore. . . . I read on and on. I hunted in the catalogue for other books by Walter Ramal. He had written one other, *Henry Brocken*."

I quote the passage from my book on Walter de la Mare, and as I do so I am reminded that though that winter afternoon seemed to me remote enough even at the time of writing (1929), ten more years have (hardly perceptibly) glided by since then. But it was on a summer afternoon, in the St. George's Café in London, that a friendship which has now lasted for the greater part of a lifetime actually began. I can remember clearly the circumstances and the scene. We met downstairs—de la Mare was waiting for me at the door —and I can remember the rather continental appearance of the room upstairs to which he took me, the clicking of dominoes. I can remember the position of our table, at which very soon we were joined by Ralph Hodgson, of whom de la Mare had just time to whisper to me that he had published a few poems here and there and was interested in dogs. Admirable qualifications! I could, I thought, have guessed about the dogs, if not about the poems. Such things leave their influence. At any rate I was not surprised; Ralph Hodgson was a person with whom I instantly felt in sympathy. He told us a dream he had had the night before. The scene was a law-court, and he was looking into the mind of an old judge who was trying an extremely intricate and difficult case—weighing every point, sifting the conflicting evidence, intensely desirous to reach the truth, to remain impartial, unswayed by prejudice either on one side or the other. And this impersonal desire to be absolutely just was somehow extraordinarily fine. The dream clearly had impressed the dreamer, and as I listened it impressed me also, for I had never had a dream of that kind.

I certainly had written *The Bracknels* at the time I am speaking of; I am not so sure about *Following Darkness*: de la Mare had written several books— three in verse and three in prose—including *The Return*. The meeting was of my seeking, and it is the only such step I have ever taken in my life— my visit to A. E. having been prompted by a quite different motive. For this I am now sorry. I should like to have met Conrad and Thomas Hardy, and so far as the latter is concerned it would have been easy enough, for I once stayed for a week within a stone's-throw of his house, Max Gate. Moreover, I had joined with a few other writers in giving him a birthday present—a first edition of Keats's *Lamia* —and had received a letter from him that would have paved the way. But the same feeling which, when I was a boy, had made it an agony to me to go to a party, was a fatal deterrent here also. I might be a nuisance, I might be unwelcome; chance encounters were all very well, but to call deliberately upon a total stranger was another proposition. True, the meeting with de la Mare had passed off all right; but then we had a great deal in common—more perhaps than any other writers of our time. My belief in his genius was absolute, and in those days it had not yet been recognized.

The St. George's Café evidently was a favourite gathering place for Georgian poets. At all events several of them were there, and Edward Thomas, who was de la Mare's great friend, sat down at our table. I have said that instinctively and at first sight I liked Ralph Hodgson; just as instinctively I did not like Edward Thomas. Hodgson struck me as completely unaffected and natural, Edward Thomas did not. There was no suggestion of dogs about *him*, I felt. He was a nature poet, but I could not even connect him with nature. I connected him with short-lived quarterlies, with the midnight oil and the labour of the file: he was languid; he was sophisticated; he was æsthetic.

Presently, to my relief, he departed, and we were
left alone to sit talking till it should be time for me
to go to my opera—*Götterdämmerung*. Richter was
conducting *Tannhäuser*, *The Meistersingers*, *Tristan*,
and two cycles of *The Ring*, and it was this, really,
that had brought me to London. Ternina was
then the great Wagnerian soprano; Van Rooy
was the best Hans Sachs I have ever heard; Van
Dyck was particularly good in *Tannhäuser*. Many
years were still to elapse before I lost my enthusiasm for German opera. It may seem odd that at
sixteen I should have been an ardent Wagnerian,
and that in middle-age I should have turned to
Verdi and the Italians, the change being usually
the other way round. But it was partly the singing
of Caruso and Bonci that converted me—and
later of Pertille and Rosa Ponselle.

My companion, however, was not interested in
opera, and we talked chiefly of writing, though of
other things too. A first conversation, when it is
to be the prelude to a friendship, has, for me at all
events, a particular *kind* of interest that makes it
different from any other. One is making dis-
coveries, and with each discovery, each recognition, there is a sense of growing intimacy: there is
more than interest, there is a sort of excitement.
Everything is unknown, experimental; it is all as
different as possible from the tranquil confidence
that follows later. I don't know whether it was on
this occasion that de la Mare told me of one of his
very first efforts—an essay on dreams. It was in

the manner of Sir Thomas Browne, written under Browne's influence, elaborate in style, and striking with its first sentence: "Whether dreams are, etc.——" the full, solemn note of seventeenth century prose. He sent it to *The Spectator*, and it was printed, but to the author's surprise among the correspondence, so that it actually appeared: "Sir:—Whether dreams are——", ending "Yours etc., Walter Ramal." Only the very young writer meets with misadventures of this kind, and they are singularly annoying at the time, even if in later life they drop into the category of amusing stories.

Our next meeting was at Anerley, though whether at the house in Worbeck Road or the house in Thornsett Road I have forgotten. Yet it must have been the latter, and I know John Freeman, another Georgian, lived close by. I remember the little garden at the back, where clock golf was laid out on a small plot of grass. It was of this garden, I think, that the lines were written:

> Breathe not—trespass not;
> Of this green and darkling spot,
> Latticed from the moon's beams,
> Perchance a distant dreamer dreams. . . .

But also perchance I am wrong, for surely, had he been there, I should have remembered the "little leaden lad" with which the poem ends.

Do houses grow like the people who inhabit them? In a tale of Hawthorne's they might; and I confess that the house at Anerley is associated in my mind with the poet who lived in it. But then even more so is Hill House at Taplow. The butler *there* might have come out of one of the stories or been put into one. When he woke me in the morning and pulled up the blinds he would inform me that the sun was shining in the garden, the dew shining on the grass, the birds singing in the trees. And, noiseless and discreet, taking away my clothes to brush them, bringing them back again, dropping a few words of conversation to show that my previous visits had not been forgotten, he would produce upon me a strange impression which I could easily have allowed to become slightly sinister. For I could not associate him with the dew or the sunlight or the birds: quite the contrary: and when at noon every day he would mount his bicycle and ride off on some mysterious errand of his own, I felt there must be more here than met the eye. True, I learned later that the purpose of these brief disappearances was connected with nothing more recondite than the backing of horses, nevertheless at the time they stimulated imagination.

And so, when de la Mare himself went to stay with Thomas Hardy, he found little things happening just as they might have happened in the novels. I recall one. When they were going out for a walk, the second wife entrusted them with flowers to be laid on the first wife's grave. Could anything be more characteristic? And I fancy that at Lamb House, Rye, the Jacobean atmosphere would have been equally perceptible, and at

Conrad's the Conradian. It is really the individuality
of the writer that impresses itself upon, that spreads
out over and colours his surroundings. There are,
too, the objects that in the passage of years he has
collected about him, all of which reflect a personal taste, while naturally one's mind is tuned
to a particular kind of receptivity. At Taplow
there was the mad cook who set fire to the house
and then carried on as usual—another character
for the stories. And there was also, in spite of
these excitements, the pervading atmosphere of
peacefulness and easiness and homeliness, in
which London seemed miles and miles away.

Into this atmosphere there plunged one afternoon an American lady journalist, bent on elicit-
ing the poet's opinions on contemporary literature. He was friendly and amused, but not very
communicative, so I supplied the opinions myself, to her increasing and scarcely veiled annoyance. He let them all pass, which annoyed her still
more, for instinctively she knew that they weren't
"the real right thing", but the views of an
obnoxious person of no importance whom he was
too lazy or too good-humoured to contradict.
I enjoyed that interview thoroughly—the only
one at which I have ever been present—and I
should have loved to see the result in cold (or
should it be warm?) American print. But doubtless she fixed it all up and gave her readers what
they expected and desired.

XIV

IT is perhaps odd that though I talked of ghosts, haunted houses, and dreams with de la Mare, this was the only side of the supernatural we discussed, yet it was not in the least this side of it which had led me to pay my visit to A. E. True, I was interested in ghosts and haunted houses, but it was the interest of curiosity. What was real and immediate was an animistic conception of nature —something that the listening spirit hears in the sound of the waves, or feels in the silence of the woods—a telepathic communication from a spirit that seemed to me both human and divine.

It had nothing to do with the weaving of tales, it was a part of my real life, therefore either it veiled some secret reality or I myself was living in a dream. It looked then, it looks now still more, as if I should never pass beyond the fringe of conjecture, but I was not satisfied, and from time to time I tried to find in the experience of others an explanation of my own. I never did find it, but, turning over a bundle of old letters from Basil de Selincourt, I can see that they reflect some such hope, though in the end this correspondence left me, as my talk with A. E. had left me, very much where I had been before. Both A. E. and de Selincourt knew exactly what they believed, had reached a position they could justify to themselves intellectually, whereas I—much less fortunate—

could evolve no creed, nor even an approxima-
tion to one. I have only one side of the correspondence to guide me, but I can guess from this
how vague and mutually contradictory my own
contributions must have been. I think probably
it all began with Mrs. de Selincourt (Anne
Douglas Sedgwick, the novelist) who had liked
Following Darkness (in fact it was she who got me
my first American publisher). Basil, at any rate,
after reviewing *The Gentle Lover*, had written to
me, and I had sent him a copy of *The Bracknels*.

The first letter to the point is from Far End,
Kingham, and is dated November 1, 1914. It
opens with a discussion of *The Bracknels* from a
literary point of view; but there is a postscript
dated three days later:

"I've been keeping this letter back, because I
was aware that there was an unanalysed residuum
of feeling in my mind connected with the element
of the supernatural so prominent in all your books.
I am not at all sure whether I have arrived at an
understanding with myself about it, but I am
conscious that there is something that does not
satisfy me, and I fancy it is this. The novel as an
art form, turns on producing the illusion of
credibility. The reader must believe that what is
described happened. In novels like yours, the
fabric depends on the pursuit of reality into the
most obscure fastnesses—your strength is in the
delicacy of your psychological analysis and the
association of unusual states of mind with unusual

impressions—of beauty, etc. In all this your success depends on the truth of your picture: you
write for readers of peculiar insight into life, and
you must carry them with you and make them to
feel you are consistently in touch with the laws
on which the life you describe, the spiritual life,
is based.

"The spiritual life has, must have, objectively a
definite substructure of some kind. We do not
know what it is, whether God, or hierarchies of
spirits, or contending spirits of good and evil, or
whether, on the other hand, it is simply its own
sanction and support. The last supposition is
ruled out surely by the dramatis personæ you
bring into action. And—this is what I am coming
to—you seem to tend to treat the question of
what the ultimate and encompassing spiritual
reality is as of less importance than the obtaining
in the novel under your hand of a particular
artistic effect. . . . I am inclined to wonder whether
the moon episode is essential to the conception of
Denis, and wonder whether you have not taken
it really as a kind of luxury of the imagination.
The book is so much an achievement that one
accepts the strange hauntings and rites almost
unmurmuringly: if they helped to the creation of
Denis, they are fully justified, but I cannot help
being a little sceptical about that; to me the direct
picture of him absolutely outsoars them."

Now here certainly one problem is touched
upon—the nature of "the encompassing spiritual

reality". If I had known that, my doubts would have been at rest, and it is the agnosticism of my attitude that de Selincourt finds unsatisfactory. But not knowing it—by which I mean not having arrived even in my own mind at any definite conclusion about it—I could only record my belief in its existence, and because I did this partly through the moon story, it does· not follow, I think, that I regarded it as of less importance than the moon story. My main object of course was to produce an artistic effect—that, I take it, was my job as an artist—but I certainly introduced nothing I did not believe in for the sake of effect: the moon story was written with the same sincerity as the descriptions of the country side. "A luxury of the imagination" perhaps, but art, or at any rate poetry, *is* a "luxury of the imagination", has its roots in emotion, intuition, vision, a soil lying below the intellect, and deeper, darker, and richer than it. To de Selincourt the art of Bach, which is almost mathematical, would have furnished a decisive refutation of this view, but the whole thing is subjective, a matter of temperament. In questions of art, I am suspicious of the intellect. Blake praised it; but, to quote the words of Arthur Symons, it is when Blake is "stammering into a speech of angels, as if just awakening out of Paradise" that he becomes a great poet, and it is when he is most intellectual that his work becomes arid and dull.

I probably defended the moon story, for in his

next letter de Selincourt says, "Your reply to
what I put forward is in one sense final. But in that
sense I did not mean to express any difference
from you. . . . On the other hand, you aim at the
spiritualisation of literature" (actually I aimed at
nothing except the expression of my individual
sense of life), "and you allow your attention to be
in part diverted by spiritual accidents, mysteries,
coincidences, details. The only abiding and sure
spiritualisation of literature lies surely in an
expansion and enlargement of the mind which
enables it to see the permeation of spiritual energy
through all things. . . . If our task here is to rise
to a perception of the whole world, all created
things, as a manifestation of the spirit, what can
be more disconcerting, what is more likely to
throw us off the true scent, than to be occupied
with partial, momentary, secondary manifestations? All such must lead away from the path of
our great spiritual conquest.

"To return more immediately to your reply to
my last letter. I entirely agree that 'it is only
through personal revelation that conviction can
ever be reached' . . . but I feel that our difference
probably lies in our conception of what the content or substance of the completest, most widely
effective revelation would be. . . . I see that to you
the spiritual at once suggests the spiritualistic,
is in close touch with the magical, operates
through a kind of sixth sense. . . . I cannot deny
that various more or less accidental evidences of

a supernatural kind have very much consolidated
my belief in a life after death, but I acknowledge
this with a good deal of regret, feeling that if I
had been completely faithful to what I have of
direct spiritual perception, I should have found
the much more fundamental security by the side of
which such things are trivial. . . . Is this power,
this perception, really conceived at its highest
when we connect it with 'dreaming', or with a
'sixth sense'? . . . To my view, your perception of
beauty in Nature and in human character is the
stronghold of your genius, and the centre of
spiritual vision in you. Your tendency to a pre-
occupation with marvels and intrusions is a
point of weakness and an embarrassment, divert-
ing you (it seems to me) from the attainment of
complete self-knowledge and retarding the natural
development and fulfilment of your powers. You
are worshipping in the side courts of the temple,
though manifestly qualified to appreciate the
greater—the un-mysterious mysteries. Yeats, it
seems to me, is eminently confined in those side
courts! and if his career has been disappointing—
and no one surely can deny it has been so—the
reason surely is that he has planted deep hopes in
shallow soil—an early crop of exquisite tendrils
and later a certain emptiness and disillusion, when
the harvest should come. . . .

"Of course you could not have written the
books you have written without having had
experiences out of the common, and your books

suggested to me that there was a sense in which it could be said you had not taken those experiences seriously enough. I had not the perspicacity to see in *what* sense; but your great devotion to art and beauty led me to think that your view might be that you used them to the full and exhausted their significance in expressing them in terms of art and beauty. . . . But I can see from your letter that my suspicion attached itself quite wrongly. At the same time what you have now written to me does not explain it away. . . . The moral sincerity you completely vindicate . . . but it is not enough for art to be morally sincere. . . . Your books and your letters both suggest a tendency towards a kind of loneliness or isolation on your part in these more spiritual experiences. It is natural indeed that that should be the case, because of their very subtlety, their incommunicability, their highly personal atmosphere. But if their full import is to be apprehended they must no doubt, more even than more normal experiences, be given their place by you in the larger contexts in which they belong. Until you are aware of some scheme of life into which you can work them, you cannot represent them except as immediate impressions: and the fact that as impressions they bear upon the aspect of reality which, whether they know it or not, concerns all men most nearly, makes the merely impressional representation of them inadequate.

"Thus, your own experience convinces you

that there exist good and evil spirits who hold inter-
course with men." (I was never, I think, so definite
as this, and had no experience at all of evil spirits.)
"But that in itself is a fact of such enormous scope
and moment that the attempt to represent it in
fiction, to place it in its setting, to describe it with
the same breath as the breakfast-table or even as
the sea and the mountains, might well break down
the whole machinery of the art. That the artist
should be faithful to the content of his own
intuition in regard to it is of course a first necessity, but it is merely the threshold. The question
next and immediately arises—into what world is
he launching us, and what knowledge, observation, etc.—parallel to what are required for presentment and understanding of daily life here—
will be required for the portrayal of this more com-
prehensive and more elusive scene?

"Your background as you present the common
affairs of life is not merely your own direct observation, but all that you have read of others' observation of the same things and all that you have
learned or inferred from conversation with others
to be their understanding of them. But has your
artistic equipment for the treatment of the other
world . . . a similar thoroughness, many-sided-
ness? Do you, in depicting the supernatural, apply
equivalent tests to assure yourself that you are
presenting objective truth? Do you not, rather,
where this largest aspect of reality is concerned,
treat your personal, untested, uncompared and so

unexplained, perhaps in some ways misinter-
preted, experience as your main subject-matter?
Here again I come back to your letter, and I seem
to find this in it—an attitude of expectancy in you
in regard to the faculty of communion with the
unseen world, a hope that intermittent glimpses
will become larger enlightenment, or a direct
manifestation of some kind. There again you
seem to me (I know most of this talk must seem
that of a fumbling outsider) to be placing your
own consciousness too high, and allowing it to
make too high a demand. Compare my own
position, for example: I have never had any
psychic experiences of any kind, but know enough
of the worship of nature you describe to be able
to enter into and understand feelings like yours,
which undoubtedly have been intenser than mine
are or ever were. I think I have always had
religious leanings, but for a number of years I
completely reconciled myself to the belief that the
whole of man's life was here before our eyes, and
that goodness, the spiritual world, was to be
found and secured in and through the materials
now available *alone*. I now feel sure that that
attitude was a reaction against the commonly
made division between this world and another. . . .
I have reverted again to a moral certainty of
immortality, and the reason is not that I can
claim any revealing experience. The reasons are
indeed so many that I could not begin to put
them down here. . . . I am convinced nothing is

too good or too wonderful to be true, and I cannot doubt at all that the meaning of life is enhanced enormously when you give it this perspective. Then finally there are on every hand these immediate psychic experiences—this dream-communion of yours with your friends is one kind. To doubt immortality begins for me to class itself among the lazinesses, the dead periods of the mind. The fact is too great to be held by normal minds steadily in view, and one could, I suppose, only live in the light of it by becoming a saint. However, whenever I turn my thoughts that way, I find it incontrovertibly there. . . . Your assurances are great relatively to mine. And if you still look forward to a revealing experience, you are probably asking for the impossible, and have therefore probably given your experience a mistaken turn. What seems to me probable is that you do not allow enough for your own extraordinary sensitiveness as a receiving instrument—for the fact, I mean, that this sensitiveness, while greatly enlarging your possible range, greatly increases the difficulty of finding and adjusting yourself to your range. It is impossible to allow too much. . . .

"I am most uncertain whether in all this I have said anything that appeals to you at all or seems to have any relevancy. I still feel moved to say something about my 'way', so far as I have found a way where Peter found none.

"Broadly speaking I have convinced myself

that we only see truly when we see everything in spiritual terms, that we are part of a developing creation in which a more and more perfect spiritual activity is to come into being, ourselves and other creatures, like or unlike ourselves, being the instruments, embodiments, substance of the great process and effort of creation. How the Creator stands to this process metaphysically I do not pretend to understand or conceive. But I assure myself of two facts:

"(1) absolute and incredible beauty is achieved in the creation, visioned extensively: it is perfected:

"(2) but there is equally a striving towards something—I can find no expression for it—wherever there is a mind.

"Here, as it were, the creative process is still going on. Perfection has not been reached. And one must realize that God is in this sense not omnipotent, that the creation of what was most worth creating—independent spiritual existences —clearly has entailed and will entail incalculable sufferings. These would have been avoided had it been possible to avoid them: it was and is impossible. They are unavoidable accompaniments of spiritual growth and may temporarily throw back the soul they exist to forward. . . . Our life on the earth is clearly a necessity to our growth. Having been sent here, our chief business is, in spirit as in body, to *be* here. . . . We have to learn what cannot be learned other-where or otherwise, and to be other-worldly in this world (whatever other world we choose) is to be in a sense stubborn, irreligious: it is the neglect of the main chance, a spiritual waste."

Now both *The Bracknels* and *Following Darkness* express the other-worldliness which is here condemned as stubborn and irreligious, and this other-worldliness is closely related to the feeling of expectancy also condemned, therefore it might be said that in a sense my question was answered. But unless it be answered in the affirmative, a question of this sort never *is* answered.

Moreover, my interest in magic and spiritualism seems to me beside the point. I admit it existed, but I had no faith in either one or the other. Nor, after this lapse of years, am I at all clear as to the nature of the psychic experiences alluded to. The term is so elastic. Wordsworth's pantheism is a psychic experience, and my own state of mind comes nearer to it than to any other I can think of. It was unaccompanied by fear, whereas the sense of human hauntings is nearly always accompanied by fear, so that the last thing desired is a revelation. The revelation I hoped for was of beauty and happiness: the other, by the very fact that its imminence creates dread, implies that it is of the nature of ugliness and gloom.

As it happens, the sense of a *human* haunting has very rarely entered my consciousness. Once I remember going, with a great friend of mine, Mrs. Frank Workman, to look at a house she was thinking of buying. The moment I crossed the threshold a feeling of intense depression descended upon me. I hated the place and advised her strongly not to take it. Later we learned that one of the bathrooms had been the scene of a singularly determined suicide. I remember, too, a house on the Antrim coast that James and I took for a month. Our housekeeper, Minnie, was with us, and two little boys, Kenneth Hamilton and Frank Campbell. I slept in the top front room, James in the room below it. Minnie's bedroom was at the back, so was Frank's, and Kenneth's was the room immediately behind mine. One morning Minnie said to me, "Do you know that that little boy, Master Kenneth, wakes up every night screaming?" I didn't know it, but the next night I heard him myself.

I lit a candle: it was between one and two in the morning; and I went to his room. I found him sitting up in bed, his eyes wide open and very bright, yet he did not see me and did not appear to be really awake. I lifted him out of the bed, carried him to my own, where I left him, and then returned to spend the remainder of the night in his. But I slept very badly, waking up again and again with the feeling that somebody else was there, yet when I lit the candle there was of course nobody. A day or two later Kenneth and Frank went out with a couple of fishermen who had offered to take them in their boat; and on their return they told an odd story. As they were

coasting along close to the shore they pointed out
the house in which they were staying. One of the
fishermen then asked which rooms they slept in,
and Kenneth said his was the back bedroom at
the top. "That," said the fisherman, "is the room
where the man cut his throat."

But Port-a-Doris, which is merely a small
lonely bay on the Donegal coast, with not a house
in sight, gave me a similar feeling of uneasiness,
of gloom and depression, and I must add that I
never learned that anything unpleasant had
happened there. In fact, it is supposed to be a most
attractive spot: nevertheless two or three minutes
of it were sufficient for me, though Stephen Gil-
bert, who was with me, felt nothing.

Now these, I am aware, hardly come into the
class of hauntings; they would find no place in
the works of F. W. H. Myers and Frank Pod-
more; they were no more than impressions of a
spiritual atmosphere that seemed to have lingered
on in a particular spot, as an odour will linger on
in a jar or a box after the object from which it
sprang has been removed. And far more often
than not such impressions reached me through
beauty. So it was at Kilwaughter Castle, which I
visited in the summer of 1927. I was very busy
just then on a book about the wood engravings
of the 'Sixties, and in the thick of my labours
received an invitation from George Buchanan to
spend a week with him at his father's house,
Kilwaughter Rectory, which is about a mile

inland from Larne. It seemed to me a capital plan; we should have the Rectory to ourselves; and I could do as much writing as I liked, because George himself, I gathered, was putting in from eight to ten hours a day on a novel. Therefore down to Larne I went.

It was perfect weather and we worked out of doors in the grounds of Kilwaughter Castle, usually by the side of a lake. Every morning after breakfast we went there, I with my notes and manuscript, George with some writing paper and a bathing suit. We sat on the shore of the lake and George thought of his novel, while I, having undertaken to deliver my manuscript by a certain date, was obliged to adopt more active methods. Kilwaughter Castle, I believe, has attracted the attention of the Society for Psychical Research, but I knew nothing of this, nor did I ever cross its doors; it was in the Archery Green beside it that I became conscious of something unusual. What that consciousness was I can best, though still unsatisfactorily, describe as a sense of the past—of the past veiled by, yet imminent in, the present. It was no more than that, yet very definite, and doubtless, working on my imagination, it was this that created a flickering, unsubstantial, and always transparent vision of a small stone building at the farther end of the Green, where certainly no building now was. Again I must call it no more than an atmosphere, but again it was confined to this one spot, and when I moved on I left it behind me, exactly as one might some low continuous sound like the droning of bees.

On the other hand, at the Rectory itself I slept in what George told me was the haunted room, and remained completely insensitive. The only hauntings reaching me there were those of the Rectory hens, who gathered outside my window in the first glimmering light to discuss the surprising advent of a new day. That nonsense at any rate I stopped. I know not why, but there is something about the average, highly-respectable hen, with her beady eye and jerky motions of the head, that exasperates me. What other creature is so fatuous, so assured of her intrinsic importance, when everybody else knows that it is only a matter of eggs? All these feathered idiots roosted in a single cabbage-shaped tree not far from the house, and of course went to bed early in order to be really fresh and active at about half-past three. It was too much! So the next night, and on every succeeding night, before retiring to my *own* bed I paid them a visit, accompanied by George, and a red setter whose name I have forgotten. We stood beneath the tree. Not a sound, not a whisper in those slumbrous branches. Being a poor sleeper myself, even this annoyed me, and I shook the branches vigorously. I cannot remember whether George helped me or not, but the setter certainly gave a yelp of delighted encouragement as a cascade of torpid fowls dropped heavily

to earth with bewildered and indignant cacklings.
Next moment he caught the idea, if not the purpose, and together we chased them over the
moonlit fields till they were out of sight. Then we
paused, wagging our tails. As for the egg-layers,
it probably took them an hour or two to realize
what had happened, and another hour to find their
way home. At all events, it was eight o'clock next
morning before they put in a subdued appearance,
late for breakfast, late for everything.

I fear I have wandered from my subject: let me
give, before finally abandoning it, one further
and more positive experience, because this time
I actually saw something.

During the years following the war I very often
went on motor tours through England with
Frank Workman and his wife. They were really
croquet tours, for we played in various tournaments, and on the occasion I have in mind we had
wound up our trip at Eastbourne. At least half a
dozen other players were stopping at the hotel
where we put up, among them E. S. Luard, who
no longer played, but was managing the tournament, a pretty big one and the last of the season.
Of course everybody in the croquet world knew
everybody else and I had often met Luard before.
He told me casually that before the end of the
tournament—which lasted for a fortnight—he
expected a visit from his grandchildren and their
parents; but I took no particular interest in the
matter.

In fact I had forgotten all about it when, a few mornings later, on coming out of my bedroom, the door of which faced Luard's own room, I saw a small boy in the passage. He was about eight or nine, dressed in a blue jersey and shorts, and he had his back turned to me, so that I did not see his face. One of the grandchildren, I surmised, and I supposed he had been paying an early visit to his grandfather and was now going down to breakfast. I followed him along the passage with the intention of making myself known to him. He turned the corner, but instead of descending the flight of stairs leading to the ground floor, he continued on his way, and I continued too. He turned the next corner—the three passages being as three sides of a square—and I was now close on his heels. I also turned the corner, and found that the passage was empty.

The child, I decided, must with remarkable celerity have nipped into the first room on either the right or the left, so I retraced my steps, and this time went downstairs. The first person I saw in the dining-room was Luard himself, having breakfast.

"I see the grandchildren have arrived," I remarked casually, but to my surprise he answered, "They haven't; I don't expect them till next week."

I said no more, for after all there was nothing to say; I had merely guessed that the little boy in the passage was one of the grandchildren, and now I found he wasn't. Nevertheless, though I haven't a notion why, I felt puzzled. The child had vanished with astonishing quickness, and now I came to think of it, I had heard no sound of an opening or closing door. I continued to ponder, with the result that after breakfast I sought out the manager of the hotel. I approached the matter with circumspection, but none the less definitely. He was equally definite. There were no children staying in the hotel. Was he sure? He was absolutely sure. Could a little boy be there without his knowledge? He could not. Then of course he asked me "Why?" I murmured something vague, and, hotel managers being adepts in the art of tact, the subject was dismissed.

Actually the only person to whom I spoke of this adventure was Mrs. Workman, but Mrs. Workman regarded me as a person to whom adventures readily happened, and wasn't so much impressed as I had expected. She even appeared to think it quite natural for me to meet in broad daylight a small boy who didn't exist, and that the only strange feature of the case was that he hadn't been accompanied by a phantom bulldog. Yet this story is true. I mean there is no vagueness, no uncertainty about it, no loophole for the entrance of imagination. I saw that little boy, pursued him, and lost him. I am not subject to hallucinations. I had no feeling of ghostliness; it was early morning; the sun was shining; and anything less ghostly than that up-to-date hotel would be difficult to conceive. I never saw my little boy again. I questioned the hall-porter and he was as positive as the manager. Moreover, what possible reason could they have for telling me lies? Perhaps there was some perfectly natural explanation, but I did not push my inquiries further. Somehow I did not want to. To drag that happy little ghost into the dubious atmosphere of psychic phenomena would have been like shutting a bird in a cage. I don't even believe he knew I was there. If he had known he would have waited for me.

But the experiences I have mentioned here were not those de Selincourt alludes to in his letters: they happened later. And they left me—even that last queer little adventure—as they found me—half convinced, half doubtful, wholly unable to attach to them any positive significance. If actually I had been a seeker of the marvellous they would have been more understandable, but I wasn't, and I mistrusted those who were. Nor had they anything to do with what I really was seeking: at least I could trace no connection; they seemed to me no more relevant to that than would have been the pranks of a poltergeist.

XV

AT the Door of the Gate was my solitary attempt to write a purely objective and realistic novel about ordinary Belfast lower-class life. The de Selincourts did not like it. They said so frankly. They thought I was writing against the grain, and Basil even broadly hinted that I should be wiser to leave it unpublished, certainly not to open my American career with it, but rather with *Following Darkness*. The American publishers, however, preferred *At the Door*, because it was new; and anyhow my American career never amounted to much, and came more or less to an end with the decisive "flop" of *Apostate*. With the exception of a few fans the American public did not want *Apostate*, and I had the odd experience of receiving a letter of apology from its publishers, which was surely very courteous of them.

As for *The Door of the Gate*, I was never to learn that anybody particularly *did* like it, and it aroused a violent animosity in Swedenborgian circles, of whose very existence, till the storm arose, I had been blissfully unaware. I fancy myself that the book contains some good passages—notably the expedition to the cemetery—but I am not going to verify this impression. My hope at the time was that the drabness and sordidness of the subject might be redeemed by distinction of style, that even a certain piquancy might emerge from the contrast, as it certainly had emerged in Henry James's *Bostonians*; but I am afraid I was too optimistic. The first and right title of the novel was *The Three Women*, and I was greatly disappointed when I discovered that this had already been used by Miss May Sinclair.

I got the right title for *The Spring Song*, however, and a much more suitable subject. Here I relinquished the attempt to be a realistic novelist treating the contemporary scene, and returned to a more restricted world. *The Spring Song* is the only one of my books about which I felt faint hopes that it might "wake up the libraries". It didn't, of course. Either the tale never found its true public, or the public disapproved of my method of presenting children. I took my young hero seriously, I presented him seriously, without any thought of the adult world. I had no secret understanding with the reader about him, and my desire was not to show him off and not to gush over him.

This young hero, Grif, in conception I suppose comes closer to Denis of *The Bracknels*, than to Tom of *Uncle Stephen* and *The Retreat*. I admit he is a little peculiar, but his contemporaries are all normal enough—even the brilliant Palmer Dorset. Palmer I thought a quite happy invention, for I had no model, though probably he is an amalgam of several boys. At any rate it amused me to write about him, so I brought him into my next book, *Pirates of the Spring*, which was called *Beach Traill* till my American publishers told me

that this would lead the reader to expect a Wild
West story.

It certainly was not that; it was in fact my only
school story. A good deal of it was written in the
open air, in Belvoir Park, where Beach lived, and
where many of the scenes are laid. It contained
no character such as Denis or Peter or Grif; the
hero was an ordinary boy—a pleasant one, I
hoped, but neither particularly clever nor particularly athletic. It seemed to me that I ought to
be able to do an ordinary boy. After all, I had
known a great number of them, and my knowledge had the advantage of being unofficial; that
is to say, not of the kind acquired through schoolmastering, or scoutmastering, or taking an interest
in boys' clubs. It owed its extensiveness indeed merely to the facts that if one boy approves of you he is apt
to introduce his friends, and that there were so many
shared interests and pursuits I had not outgrown.

Pirates I enjoyed writing, but by the world in
general I suspect it was regarded as a "juvenile".
It wasn't; it was a perfectly serious novel; and
actually it found a champion in a most unexpected
quarter. Susan Mitchell gave it an extraordinarily
sympathetic and understanding review—one of
the best I have ever received for anything. But
then Susan was very much my kind of person;
which I expect is more help with my kind of book
than with most.

At this time she was assisting A. E. to edit *The
Irish Statesman*, and it was in my capacity as a

regular contributor to *The Statesman* that I first made her acquaintance. Without any preliminaries we became friends. True, we quarrelled perpetually about proofs: I simply *couldn't* get her to send me the proofs of my articles. This worried me, because the printers were far from brilliant, and I hate mistakes. Susan thought me morbidly particular. After a vigorous dust-up she'd promise faithfully to send me the next proof, but in the end she'd nearly always correct it herself. I didn't mind so much about reviews, but I did mind about "middles". Yet nobody else, it appeared, wanted proofs, so under the plea of saving time, though really in a spirit of obstinacy, she'd do them, hope for the best, and then be terrified if there was a misprint. Needless to say, there always *were* misprints. She even admitted that there were more in my articles than in those of anybody else, but then, as she speciously added, this was because I made her so nervous that she couldn't read them properly. On one occasion the very lines got mixed up, so that whatever interest the thing may have aroused was rather of a crossword or jigsaw nature than literary. This accident, Susan declared, had happened after the proof—particularly carefully corrected—had been returned to the printer. What could she do, therefore, except refrain from sending me a copy of the paper—a course she had considered until she remembered that, with my fussiness, I'd be certain to write and demand explanations.

When she came to see me in Belfast I took her round all my favourite haunts—Belvoir, the Lagan, the Moat. And we chattered as happily as two schoolboys—with the same queer sudden interruptions of argument and contradiction. Susan denied that she had any literary sense, which of course wasn't true, though her taste had its oddities. She liked my books, but her favourite novel was *The Wide Wide World*, which she was always wanting me to read, and upon which she would discourse as if it had been a work by Flaubert. She had charm, she had intelligence, she had wit, she was a very loyal and delightful friend. I liked her extremely, and sometimes I wondered how it was that women of that sort so frequently remain unmarried. It was not that they lacked femininity; nobody could have been more feminine than Susan.

After *Pirates* I definitely knew the kind of novel I wished to write, so that *Pender Among the Residents*, my next book, seems to me a throw-back, breaking the sequence which, but for that, continues to the end. I do not mean that in the composition of *Pender* I was thinking primarily of "what the public wants", but I certainly was telling a story that had for me much less personal significance than any of its successors and than several of its predecessors. It had not come to me; I had invented it, planned it out, I had felt no compulsion to write it: in a word it was professional. I do not mean by this that it was hasty or scamped work; I do mean, however, that it was a manufactured book, had no compelling urge behind it. It is to professionalism that we owe *The Hand of Ethelberta*, *A Laodicean*, and *The Well Beloved*; *Chance*, and *The Arrow of Gold*. And personally I feel that we could have done very well without any of these, though I know it was *Chance* that brought Conrad his vogue.

Pender was not likely to bring anybody a vogue. It is a composite tale. There is a village chronicle intended to be light and amusing; there is a rather conventional ghost story, which I don't imagine can be at all successful, since I never really believed in it, as I did in the experiences of Denis and Peter and Grif; and there is Trefusis, an imaginary portrait of that delectable infant phenomenon, Master Romney Robinson. I hoped it might prove readable, but from the point of view of these notes *Pender* definitely is negligible —a social comedy with a happy ending. It was with a sense of relief, and in a totally different spirit, that I approached my next book. Here the subject suited me, ingenuity and invention were not required; the story was there, and success or failure, it seemed to me, depended wholly on the faithfulness of the presentment.

XVI

ONCE I had thought of it, I wondered that I had not thought of it sooner. I happened to be in London at the time, and got a note from Michael Sadleir asking me to call to see him at Constable's. So round I went to Orange Street, and to my astonishment Sadleir's first words were that he had heard I intended to write an autobiography and that they would like to publish it. Now I hadn't yet written a line, nor could I remember having mentioned the plan to anybody, but the immediate result was that *Apostate* there and then passed out of the realm of contemplation into that of a work on the stocks.

On returning to Ireland I began to write it, and never had anything come so easily: it seemed almost to write itself. Later I tried out three or four chapters in *The Saturday Westminster* and elsewhere, but I was to regret this, for when the book was finished de la Mare, unknown to me, passed on the manuscript to Sir John Squire, who said he would have published the whole thing as a serial in *The London Mercury* if these chapters had not already appeared.

As a matter of fact the idea of serialization *had* occurred to me, when I was about half-way through my task, but the paper I thought of was *The Irish Statesman*. And it must have been to

Susan, not to A. E., that I broached the subject, as the following letter shows.

My dear Forrest Reid,

I need not say I like the sample of the book. I felt inclined when I read it to shout aloud my appreciation, and did——to A. E. I never came across a story so beautifully handled as regards the youth in it. I cannot go into details of the treatment, I haven't the skill—or the cheek. I only know it is a book I would like to have by me—as a retreat for my fretted soul. The beautiful country you lived in as a boy—the world inside this world—struck me very much. The country *I* have inside myself or in dreams is nothing like so spiritual. I have only clearly realised that I have such a place lately, but alas in it people give garden parties, and there are rectors and curates, and the parties are uproariously merry, and I am delighted with the merriment and very loath to leave it.

The only jarring passage in the book is the story of the English boy's girl cousin. I would hate that naturally, I have such a prunes and prisms mind. I'd be sure to pick that out for a stone of stumbling, or rather my wobbly mind would be attracted to it as the wobbly bicyclist to the stone in the road.

I love Emma. She is greater than Nan, who brought us up, and Nan was very great. I think you are writing a book that will be a haven of delight to many. Go on and finish it.

But serials don't seem to suit the *Statesman*. We tried James Stephens' *In Tir na n'Og*, and our readers objected. This is an inadequate letter, but I felt shy of tearing into its component parts a whole which delighted me beyond possibility of criticism. The *way* you go back is so admirable.

I grieve you should have rheumatism and yet have to take in the milk. Jenny, my sister, and I used to do it. Now we have a house and a maid and not half the zest for the milk we had in servantless days. All the same, a wife would be a sound investment in view of the rheumatism. Get one that has been inoculated with anti-rheumatic serum.

Yours ever,

SUSAN MITCHELL.

I finished *Apostate*, and towards the end of it I described an experience or adventure that happened to me shortly before my seventeenth birthday. As it has never ceased to be relevant perhaps I may be pardoned for reproducing the passage.

"It was June, and I was supposed to be working for an Intermediate examination, and had a book or two with me even on this blazing afternoon. It was hot and still. The breathless silence seemed unnatural; seemed, as I lay motionless in the tangled grass, like a bridge that reached straight back into the heart of some dim antiquity. I had a feeling of uneasiness, of unrest, though I lay so still—of longing and excitement and expectation: I had a feeling that some veil might be drawn away, that there might come to me something, some one, the Megistos Kouros perhaps, either with the winged feet of Hermes, or the thyrsos of Dionysos, or maybe only hairy-shanked Pan of the Goats. My state of mind just then was indistinguishable from that of the worshipper. . . . I was certainly prepared to join in whatever rites or revels might be required. My body seemed preternaturally sensitive, my blood moved quickly, I had an extraordinary feeling of struggle, as if some power were struggling to reach me as I was trying to reach it, as if there *was* something there, something waiting, if only I could get through. At that moment I longed for a sign, some definite and direct response, with a longing that was a kind of prayer. And a strange thing happened. For though there was no wind, a little green leafy branch was snapped off from the tree above me, and fell to the ground at my hand. I drew my breath quickly; there was a drumming in my ears; I knew that the green woodland before me was going to split asunder, to swing back on either side like two great painted doors. . . . And then—then I hesitated, blundered, drew back, failed."

While I was writing these words the whole incident seemed to happen over again, was renewed so vividly in memory that the tree was growing in my room, and I could feel the hot sunshine on my hands and body. Now, the next book I wrote was *Demophon*. It was a kind of adventure story, with the scene laid in an ancient and imaginary Greece. But it has been pointed out to me that though the setting and incidents are so different, a remarkable likeness exists between *Demophon* and *Apostate*. Demophon is the boy in *Apostate*, Demeter is Emma, Hermes is the dream-playmate.

All this was pure coincidence, however, and what I am leading up to is only my persuasion that with the writing of *Demophon* the nameless spirit of *Apostate* had become Hermes.

Why? I did not know why. There was no discoverable reason. Yet in my mind the identification had taken place, and was to remain. I knew little of Hermes. The Homeric Hymn did not fit in with my conception of him, and there seemed indeed little to be known. He was the guide of souls; he was a God of dreams, and also a boy God—a protector of boys, whose image was set up in the corners of playgrounds and gymnasiums: there was the lovely statue of Praxiteles. But compared with Apollo, with Pan, with Dionysos, what a slender part this God had played in Greek mythology and legend! I could find no authoritative account of a cult of Hermes in the past, though so much had been written of the cults of other divinities. Yet there must have been one, and it was now lost, forgotten. Still, the spirit I had prayed to in my boyhood had been a nameless spirit, therefore why should he now have

assumed a name and a form, so that late at night
I wrote the last words of *Demophon* with a strange
emotion and excitement, a persuasion that some
intelligence outside my own was impressing itself upon me?

I am not producing all this as the preface to a
confession of faith. It is a confession of *something*,
nevertheless: call it the acceptance of an imaginative symbol projected from an unknown spiritual
energy. It is not faith, because it will not bear the
test of unhappiness: it comes, rather, *with* happiness,
and in the hour of loneliness and loss would have
no power to console. It is not constant, yet it is
persistent in the sense that it is recurrent. On the
other hand, it is more in the nature of a desire, and
acquires reality only when one is half in the dream
world, and at the first contact with the bitterness
of pain and disappointment would vanish. It is
the accompaniment of Tom's affection for Uncle
Stephen, but it could not have comforted him, it
would itself have failed, had Uncle Stephen failed
him.

Nevertheless, the obstinacy with which it
haunted my mind caused me to wonder if it had
not its origin in some universal spiritual force from
which Christianity and all religions had sprung.
I knew that to the orthodox Protestant it would
appear merely a childish superstition, but the
Catholic mind is more understanding, less sceptical, so I wrote to André Raffalovich, with whom
I had kept up an odd kind of friendship—entirely

by correspondence—ever since the days of *The Kingdom of Twilight*. Had he refused to take my letter seriously it would neither have surprised nor offended me, but he did not do so, though he would not answer on his own authority. I give therefore the verdict of the Catholic Church as transcribed by him. He does not name the author of the judgement; from whom, likewise, he would seem to have withheld my own name.

"Your friend can find in his Hermes whatever spirit he likes to evolve out of his hungers and desires, and this ideal of his (in so far as it consorts with the ideals painted for us in the New Testament) is no doubt the same spiritual ideal as you have found in Christ, or rather one facet of it. Unhappily I know nothing of his Hermes, so that I don't know what his ideals signify: but it is clear that Christ is the fulfilment of all our earlier hopes and the reality of our later dreams, so that there, in Christ, all religions touch hands. But it is only His own revelation to us of Himself and of God that gives us *fully* the meaning and reality of our hopes and hungers. Yet though His revelation is as complete as can be, our apprehension of it is not complete. We see darkly, and that in a mirror."

The rest of the communication is largely repetitive, and I took the answer to be that along my own particular path I need hope to advance no further, and that until I abandoned it for the Church's way I should remain in darkness.

"Christ enlighteneth every man that cometh into the world" my unknown counsellor quotes, "because we were made for Christ, and therefore search for Him, because we lack Him and need Him."

But was I made for him? It was clear, at all events, that to the Christian mind I was clinging obstinately and wilfully to an outworn creed, when all I had to do was to accept the light and the truth. The French novelist François Mauriac had already told me this in even plainer terms, and had found in my spiritual and mental outlook "le vide effroyable que creuse dans les êtres l'absence de Dieu". It did not satisfy me. It did not impress me to be told that "Christ enlighteneth every man that cometh into the world" if I felt he had not enlightened me. As I have said, I believe, with Socrates, that we can only really love what is good, but it would be as idle to pretend that the spirit hovering before my imagination in the least resembled Christ, as to affirm that among our earthly friends we must all feel drawn towards and love the same person. The spirit I searched for was a spirit of nature—a god, but not God, not the creator and controller of the universe. The statement that I must see him as Christ would, it seemed to me, be exactly paralleled were I to insist that the Christian must see Christ as him. Translated into the Christian mythology he would be much more like the angel who accompanies the youthful Tobias on his adventures.

What follows will, I know, seem childishly fantastical, but it naturally comes in here, and it happened. It is concerned with a prayer, though I am afraid there was nothing spiritual about the prayer; in fact it was the kind of prayer one makes when one is the age of Huckleberry Finn: "She told me to pray every day, and whatever I asked for I would get it. But it warn't so. Once I got a fish-line, but no hooks. I tried for the hooks three or four times, but somehow I couldn't make it work. By-and-by, one day, I asked Miss Watson to try for me, but she said I was a fool." Now I have no doubt that Miss Watson would have said the same thing to me, though to all appearances I did make it work—far too well. I had been worried for some weeks by the persistent yapping of a small hysterical dog, who was turned out of his home every morning after breakfast, and between that hour and lunch time never ceased to bark, whether or not there was anybody or anything to bark at. In the end this got so much upon my nerves that I asked the dog's owner to keep him in the house in the mornings and put him out in the afternoons instead, when I was not working. This was promised, but the promise was not kept, and in an hour of extreme exasperation I put up my petition—in all seriousness—that the annoyance might cease. And I put it to my own god.

On next morning and the next there was no barking, and I thought it only civil to express my

thanks to the human agent. But I was informed
that the dog had not been kept in the house as I had
supposed; on the contrary, on the morning after
my prayer he had been turned out as usual, and
had run straight on down to the main road where
he had been run over—or, as his owner put it,
cut in two by a tram. Take it as a coincidence, I
was none the less shocked, for instantly I remembered the part I had played. I must add in self-
defence that the ruthless form of the removal was
not what I had contemplated. On the other hand,
the removal was all I *had* contemplated, which
perhaps invalidates the excuse.

XVII

BEFORE proceeding further it might be well,
I think, to consider here certain aspects of
that second life which, even if we attach no significance to it, is lived by all of us in dreamland. The
pertinence of this will, I trust, become clear later;
for the moment I shall but ask a few questions,
hazarding now and then an answer that I admit
will be a guess, for this is a subject upon which—
in spite of psycho-analysis—nobody really knows
very much.

Why is it that, though the moral and critical
senses on the whole appear to be lowered in sleep,
the mind and memory frequently become more
alert? One may say that the former are acquired qualities, created by education, emulation, imitation,
and therefore more readily suffer an eclipse, but this
does not explain the stimulation of the latter, nor
account for the erratic nature of their working.
Let me give one remarkable example of the
activity of the dream memory, which occurred
when I was an apprentice at Musgrave's, and as
testimony has the possible advantage that the
person concerned did not realize its strangeness,
was not in the least interested in such matters, in
fact regarded it merely as a stroke of good fortune. It was after stock-taking, when the books
were balanced at the end of our financial year—
the actual date being the first of May. On this

occasion they would not balance; there was a trifling error—only of some few shillings—but it was untraceable, and worried the book-keeper so much that he worked late night after night, in solitude, under murmuring gas-jets, watched by puzzled mice who could not understand this intrusion. He went over cash books and ledgers, checking entries and figures that he had checked twenty times before, but always he arrived at the same disappointing result. This continued for several weeks, and anybody else would have given up the task, for actually the mistake did not matter. Indeed, it need never have been mentioned. Musgrave's was an old-fashioned firm, and no accountants were brought in to audit books and ask questions. But it put our friend on his mettle; he regarded it as a challenge; it haunted his mind; and the fact of its intrinsic unimportance made no difference. Now he was a person far from robust at any time, and after this prolonged period of extra labour he went home one night so exhausted that when he sat down in a chair to take off his boots, instead of doing so he promptly fell asleep. In this sleep he had a dream, and in this dream he was not carrying on his search, he was simply, in the ordinary way, making an entry in the petty-cash book. But he was making it, as he suddenly saw, on the wrong side. Then he noted the date and the number of the page and awoke.

That there was anything odd in this noting of the page number and the date (some six months

earlier) did not appear to strike him even later
when he was telling me about it. To me it remains
inexplicable, for if in his dream he was conscious
that the entry was wrong, why did he not correct
it? He awoke cold and dead tired, but though it
was long past midnight and the trams had stopped
running he was not content to wait till morning,
but put on his hat and coat and tramped back into
town. He unlocked the front door and entered
the dark silent building; he unlocked the safe; he
took out the cash book and opened it at the page
memorized in his dream—and there before his
eyes, sure enough, was the wrong entry—debit
where it should have been credit, or vice versa.
His pleasure when he recounted this adventure
next morning seemed almost to compensate for
all the tedious hours of worry and extra work;
the peculiar *nature* of the experience, on the other
hand, had not impressed him; it was no more than
luck—fortunate, but no more remarkable than
might have been the catching of a train for which
one should have arrived a few minutes late.

I have never had a dream like this. My nearest
approach to it is so feeble in comparison that I
only record it because it has another significance.
It happened years ago, after I had been listening
to a Chopin recital given by Pachmann. He had
played amongst many other things a prelude
that I did not know, and the tune of which I
tried vainly to remember on my way home. I
dare say it would have come back to me eventu-

ally, but actually I had not to wait. Most kindly that very night he played it to me over again while I was asleep, and in the morning it was fixed clearly in my mind.

I mention this, I say, only because it raises a further point—a point also suggested by another dream, in which I read with absorbed fascination the first chapter of a quite imaginary new novel by Conrad. It was in his earlier and more exotic manner, filled with the sleepy brooding atmosphere of *Heart of Darkness*, and the hero was a Roman Catholic priest who had got into trouble at home and had drifted out to the Islands. The exact nature of the trouble had not yet been revealed when I woke up.

The point I refer to, however, is the question of time in dreams, of their actual duration. Andrew Lang, who was not himself, I should think, much of a dreamer, but was extremely learned in all such matters, seems inclined to the view that dreams are instantaneous. In support of this, in *Longman's Magazine* (Vol. XL: page 484), he cites the remarkable dream of Alfred Maury—remarkable because here for once we happen to have an independent witness, in the person of Maury's mother. Madame Maury, who for some reason had come into her son's bedroom, saw a thin wooden lath fall from the top of the bed and strike Alfred's neck, immediately awakening him. Yet in that instant of awaking, the sleeper, feeling the blow, had composed a whole drama to explain it—a drama in which, suspected by the tribunal of the French Revolution, he was arrested, tried, condemned, taken to the place of execution and guillotined.

On the face of it, this seems conclusive, but there is another view, of which Andrew Lang had never heard, since it was first expressed, I think, only a few years ago, by J. W. Dunne. According to Dunne, the dream consciousness wanders as freely in the future as in the past, and the dreamer, having knowledge of the future, would know that he was going to be struck by the falling lath, and simply invent a plot that would lead logically up to the final incident of the blow that awakened him. I confess that, in spite of its ingeniousness and plausibility, I am more interested in this theory than convinced by it. If the dreamer knew about the blow, why should he not accept it as it actually happened, why should he transform the lath into a guillotine? Yet if we reject Mr. Dunne's explanation it would seem that the dream must have been instantaneous. Does it, however, follow that all dreams must be instantaneous? I am convinced that the vast majority are not. How, for example, could I get an instantaneous impression of Pachmann's playing of that Chopin prelude, when for me the chief feature of his playing was its caressing quality, the lingering on certain notes, the pauses *before* certain notes, so that the ear divined them before the sound actually reached it? And the Conrad dream is in the same category. Literature has always appealed to me as a deeper, richer form of music, and my pleasure in it is taken slowly. In this case that pleasure was created largely by the long-drawn cadences of the Conrad rhythm, which I probably accentuated, since I never read anything I really care for without sounding every syllable. Besides, I have watched and listened to my own bulldogs, Pan and Remus, dreaming, and the dream adventure, whatever it may have been, obviously extended over a period of several minutes.

It is a question upon which few writers seem to have reached the same conclusion. Stevenson, who found many incidents for his fictions in dreams, and dreamed two of the scenes in *Jekyll and Hyde*, thinks that "time goes quicker in the life of dreams, some seven hours to one"; Dickens has a different measure. But clearly these are only guesses, and actually we do not know. I should think myself that there is no fixed measure. Time in dreams is as mysterious as is everything else in them, and our very dream faculties work inconsistently. There are dreams in which everything proceeds perfectly rationally, humdrum realistic dreams; and there are others in which our sense of values is completely altered —in which words, images, happenings acquire a profound emotional quality, a terror or a beauty that in waking life no intellectual analysis can explain. To-night's dream may be soberly commonplace, last night's the wildest phantasmagoria. And occasionally one passes into the other.

o

Certain dreams undoubtedly suggest the hallucinations of insanity, just as there is a form of
insanity that suggests a prolongation of the dream
state. A "dreamy" poem is not at all the same
thing as a dream poem. In the true dream poem
the word "dream" never occurs, because the
consciousness of dreaming is not there. The
Chimères of Gérard de Nerval were written when
he was mad, but they are definitely dream poems,
and suggest that the madness itself was a dreaming
from which he could not be awakened. Thus even
the sanest of us hover in sleep between sanity and
insanity—for is not one of the properties of
sanity simply the capacity to shake off the visions
of the night? Here is Gérard's mysterious *Artémis:*

> La Treizième revient. . . . C'est encor la première;
> Et c'est toujours la seule,—ou c'est le seul moment:
> Car es-tu reine, ô toi! la première ou dernière?
> Es-tu roi, toi le seul ou le dernier amant? . . .
>
> Aimez qui vous aima du berceau dans la bière;
> Celle que j'aimai seul m'aime encor tendrement;
> C'est la mort—ou la morte. . . . O délice! ô tourment!
> La Rose qu'elle tient, c'est la *Rose trémière*.
>
> Sainte napolitaine aux mains pleines de feux,
> Rose au cœur violet, fleur de sainte Gudule:
> As-tu trouvé ta croix dans le désert des cieux?
>
> Roses blanches, tombez! vous insultez nos dieux:
> Tombez, fantômes blancs, de votre ciel qui brûle:
> —La sainte de l'abîme est plus sainte à mes yeux!

Can we say what it means? Yet its obscurity is
not the obscurity fashionable to-day, which after

all is largely a form of poetic diction, though not the poetic diction Wordsworth fought so hard to get rid of. The poem stirs something in the darkness below consciousness, but does not quite awaken it. It comes to us, a whisper out of the unknown; "then darkness again, and a silence". What significance did Gérard attach to the *Rose tremière* that he writes it in italics? It is the kind of poetry I particularly like, but carried here beyond my range of receptivity. True, I get a poem, I get beauty, I get what Yeats says poetry essentially is—"a touch from behind a curtain", but the vision, dazzlingly clear and bathed in light, that was Gérard's, escapes me. Nevertheless, if we know something of the tragic facts of his life, we seem to find a vague relation to them. There is the favourite doctrine of reincarnation; there is the haunting memory of a lost love of youth, who returns under many disguises: "I am the same as Mary, the same as your mother, the same as she whom under many forms you have always loved. At each of your trials I have dropped one of the masks with which I veil my face: soon you will see me as I am."

Dreaming, we are more susceptible to, more defenceless against, both happy and unhappy influences. But *what* is it that has this power over us? Not long ago I had a dream in which nothing happened; I was simply alone in a very ordinary room; and yet I awoke in a sweat of terror. It seems clear that the real dream had not even

commenced; but the shadowy agent controlling
it had prepared his atmosphere, was just warming
to his task when I awoke. So a dream may have a
particular significance for the dreamer which it
has not for others. In Walter de la Mare's dream
story, *The Wharf*, for instance, I could feel none
of the sense of horror which obviously it had
aroused in the author. I read it calmly: it com-
municated no shudder; in short I missed it.

To me dreams which have a directly physical
origin seem to be of a different kind from those
that float up out of the subconscious, and to come
closer to the symptoms of a fever or an indiges-
tion. Of such Sir Thomas Browne says, "Cato,
who doted upon cabbage, might find the crude
effects thereof in his sleep." And again, it is of
this kind of dream he is thinking when he writes:
"To add unto the delusion of dreams, the fantastical objects seem greater than they are; and
being beheld in the vaporous state of sleep, en-
large their diameter unto us. Democritus might
seldom dream of atoms, who so often thought of
them. He almost might dream himself a bubble
extending unto the eighth sphere."

Stevenson, writing of the dreams that troubled
him in boyhood, tells how "the room swelled and
shrank, and my clothes, hanging on a nail, now
loomed up instant to the bigness of a church, and
now drew away into a horror of infinite distance
and infinite littleness."

I have a friend who suffered much from this

type of dream in boyhood, but has since grown
out of it. Yet at school he kept an electric torch
under his pillow, because gazing into its light
helped to banish the hallucination that still persisted after he had awakened. To me it is doubtful
if this is really dreaming. Rather, it seems a
pathological state between sleeping and waking,
in which the senses temporarily are disoriented.
Intrinsically there is no horror in the idea of ex-
panding and contracting objects, the horror exists
only for the dreamer, who finds himself in an
abnormal world which he half recognizes as
insane yet from which he cannot escape. And it
is, I suspect, the mental struggle that produces
anguish, and if there were no struggle, there
would be merely a fantastical picture that might
inspire curiosity but scarcely fear.

Dreams, I fancy, change in accordance with the
stratum of sleep which the sleeper has reached. I
have known a dream to begin terrifyingly, and
then, altering its course, become increasingly
commonplace before emerging finally into the
friendly light of day. One may even make an
appeal in a dream of this indeterminate nature,
and in my experience it invariably meets with a
kindly response. Charles Lamb describes a dream
he had after reading a poem of Barry Cornwall's—
a dream beginning most promisingly, but ending,
very much to his disappointment, in this kind of
anti-climax. The most priceless example, however,
is the dream of the Scotch professor, as narrated

by Andrew Lang. "He dreamed that the Night-hag came to him, the Mother of all Nightmares. She squirmed upwards like a black, poisonous, personal smoke from the earth. She filled all the world with the horror of her wings, her fangs, her claws, her coils. The professor went for her like a man, got her by the throat, gripped with her, and had the pleasure of seeing her dwindle and diminish, till she was a mere shadow of herself. Then she spoke, and said in a thin whisper—'Won't you at least give me a testimonial?' "

Can we dream of what has never entered our waking consciousness even as the most fugitive thought or feeling? I have been assured that we can, but I very much doubt it. What were the dreams that Coleridge only hints at in *The Pains of Sleep*? However monstrous the growth—and I have had dreams myself that nothing would induce me to record—the seed, I fancy, lies dormant in the mind of the dreamer. To pass from fact to fiction, I remember reading, many years ago, a novel by W. D. Howells, in which a man dreams that his wife has been unfaithful to him with his most intimate friend. The instant he awakens he tries to forget this poisonous fabrication, but he cannot; it eats into his mind like a cancer, and at last becomes an obsession. It was a gloomy and powerful tale (*The Shadow of a Dream*), and the fact that Howells should have chosen a theme so extraordinarily unlike those he usually treated, suggests that it was not invented, but was an elaboration of an actual experience he had heard of. But my point is, *Could* the dream have entered a mind not already tainted by jealousy? Howells thinks so: I do not.

All this is less a digression than it must appear to be. I am approaching my main subject steadily if slowly, and I could only approach it in this fashion. Our dreams must owe something to our daily occupations, therefore a writer probably will dream more in words than do those who do not write, and I should think it likely that a Verdi or a Beethoven must frequently compose a tune in his sleep. The very brevity of the composition would here be an assistance, for the dream collaborator (whom we are at last approaching) soon tires, and often is content with striking little more than an opening phrase. One awakens, and above the drowsy surface of consciousness there floats a vanishing impression that creates no more than a faint ripple, like that caused by an invisible swimmer, some small amphibious creature crossing a pond from bank to bank.

If it be more than this it will be well to write it down immediately, for nocturnal impressions fade far more rapidly than do those received in daytime. They are so vivid at the moment that we imagine a few words will be sufficient to recapture them at a later date, but it is not so. Thus, turning over a box of ancient notes, I find the following cryptic sentences, which certainly at the time seemed to me to convey all that was necessary.

"Story of a house haunted by the man *himself*. Lost river, and contracting garden."

Not even the dimmest notion of what this story was to be is now recoverable, yet when the note was made it must have been so clearly in my mind that fourteen words appeared to be a sufficient epitome. They are not. Instead, I ask myself how can a river be lost, or a garden change its size? Both questions are difficult to answer, and in any case what have they to do with a man who haunts his own house? Again, is the haunter actually a ghost bound to the house he once lived in, or is it the ghost of the child or boy he had been, who returns to this man in middle age? "What song the Syrens sang, or what name Achilles assumed when he hid himself among women, though puzzling questions, are not beyond all conjecture." *My* story is—and all because I was too lazy——

But no, I don't really suppose that the world has lost much by my indolence. On the other hand, I should be surprised if it had not lost a great deal by the indolence of Coleridge—a dreamer of rarer dreams. He himself is silent on the point, and the solitary example recorded was lost not through indolence but interruption. Probably among the least loved figures in all history may be ranked the anonymous "person on business from Porlock". How evocative are the five words! I picture him a Nonconformist of serious mind and oozing respectability; clothed in black and carrying, I know not why, a small leather handbag. Yet I have a feeble and sneaking sympathy with him, for what, after all, was his crime? Merely that he interrupted Coleridge when the latter happened to be writing out a poem composed in sleep. The interview lasted "above an hour"—interviews with Coleridge inevitably would—and when it was over the poem had vanished beyond recall. Unfortunately this particular poem was not *France: an Ode*, but *Kubla Khan*—one of the loveliest things ever written. Yet Coleridge had left other poems unfinished. "Encinctured with a twine of leaves" is even lovelier, and no "person from Porlock" can be blamed for the fact that it remains a fragment. Only the first stanza was written down, and the bewildering reason given for this flash of energy is that the poet "wished to obtain a friend's judgement on the metre". I find this unconvincing. The lines are clearly a dream poem—I could absolutely swear to that. Coleridge dreamed it and let it go. That is, if there ever *was* anything more. I am doubtful; as I am doubtful about the unwritten portion of *Kubla Khan*. One thing is certain—that the dream inspiration must be utilized without delay; otherwise it will fade out, "pass away, like a rainbow, or the glories of the evening sky".

For even the expanded, the more carefully recorded dream adventure loses its fragrance and colour more rapidly than a flower dried between the pages of a book. Its charm also, the peculiar quality that gave it a meaning independent of logic. Here, for instance, is a fuller note. It has no title, but is simply headed, *Time Story*. "A small boy has been sent to the house of some friends, taking with him, as a present, his own photograph. He is in a room with a grown-up girl, and they are going out somewhere together. From the window he has a view of an old church standing in a square, of a river with a stone bridge spanning it, and of a number of old-fashioned, gabled houses. It is a country town, and there are red roofs and green roofs, latticed windows, and pigeons. The sun is setting. Presently they go out, but he lags behind his friend, and when he turns the corner of the square she has vanished. Moreover, he has now forgotten where they were going. He turns back, seeking the house they have left, but cannot find the way, for everything has altered. There are more houses, more streets, than there should be. The town has grown modern and strange: the streets are crowded with people. He asks his way, but when at length he reaches the house he is seeking and knocks at the door, it is opened by a maid who is a stranger to him. Once again he is shown into the room from which he had stood looking out with the girl, but the prospect is altered, and even the furniture in the room is different. Alone in the room, he wanders about uneasily between the window and the fireplace, and finally, sitting down at a table, begins to turn over the pages of a photograph album.

Suddenly he comes upon the photograph he had brought as a present, only now it is faded and discoloured, and he realizes that it must have been taken years and years ago. He has a feeling of dizziness, and then once more he is standing by the window looking out, and the girl is saying, 'So you've brought me your photograph! What a nice present, and what a kind little boy you are!' "

This shows the dream collaborator in a pretty lazy mood, but I have quoted it because it illustrates his strange power of persuasion. Obviously he bamboozled me into the belief that here was a story worth noting, and I took the note while the illusion was still fresh. Now I can make little of it: cannot transpose it back into its own world. The story depends on a certain atmosphere and emotion that I myself, being the little boy, supplied at the time, but that I should now have to invent. All that remains is a jumble of shifting unsubstantial images whose significance is lost.

I have many such notes for stories, a few of them eventually became stories, and all originated in dreams that seemed to me at the time possible to utilize. Yet I have never actually dreamed of writing. The nearest approach to this I have made was the reading over of what apparently I *had* written. In the dream I received by post the proof sheets of a novel, and sat down to correct them. And the further I read, the less I liked this novel, which was entitled *The World*. The title was surprising, the novel was more surprising still, and the fact that I couldn't remember having written a line of it was most surprising of all. In the end it produced upon me so sinister an effect that I awoke as from a nightmare.

A curious feature of the dream collaborator is that he seems quite indifferent to his material— almost anything will suffice. Indeed, as an artist, like Henry James he appears to be stimulated by the very difficulties to be overcome, though his method of solution is usually to ignore them. But he is not really an artist, for it is just where the artist would be most meticulous that *he* is most careless. He is prodigal of fragments, good at introductory scenes, can find eternity in a grain of sand, but anything will distract his attention and start him off on a fresh tack. Here is such a tangled dream adventure that befell me recently. It seemed to me that it was morning and that it was time to get up. I went from my bedroom to the bathroom, and found lying on the floor there the two pieces of a tortoise-shell comb that had been broken in half. After bathing and shaving I returned to my bedroom, and here again, on the floor, was a broken comb, but this time the two pieces had been placed carefully side by side. I saw now that these were no accidents, but were designed to attract my attention, and had a mysterious meaning. When I had finished dressing I went downstairs and out into the open

air, but not into the familiar scene of Ormiston
Crescent, though the house had been the Ormiston Crescent house. With the closing of the door
it had vanished, all houses had vanished, I was in
the midst of a park-like country, green and fresh
and bathed in sunlight. I walked on over the dewy
grass, and there was a sound of water, of running
water, as from a hidden stream. Then, floating in
the air about five feet above the ground, I saw
a little boy. He could not have been more
than seven or eight, and he was asleep, lying in
the air horizontally, poised there like a small angel
on a cloud, but at a slight angle, his head and
shoulders being slightly higher than his feet; in
fact he was in the position of being carried, and,
accepting this suggestion, I placed my arms beneath him, which must have been what was intended, for instantly I felt him grip me round my
neck and shoulder, though he did not awaken. I
noticed now that he was suspended in the air by a
thin, nearly invisible cord. This cord, moreover,
was being gently drawn in, like a fishing line, and
following the direction of the pull I crossed the
grass to the steps of a tower. The pull was very
feeble, but it was now upward, and after climbing
a few steps I stopped, and began myself to pull
in the contrary direction. Immediately there was a
commotion above, and I heard angry voices, and
one voice in particular crying out, "He'll drown
the princess: the princess will be drowned."

Simultaneously I perceived that I and the sleep-

ing boy and the country we were in were all at the
bottom of a lake, through whose clear waters the
tower rose into an upper world. The pull against
me still continued, though it was growing weaker,
and I now saw the face of a flushed and panting
little girl who was struggling in the water,
through which I was pulling her down.

I stood still, and a number of agitated young
men came running down the steps of the tower.
"You've drowned the princess," they told me
angrily, and one seemed on the point of attacking
me, while the others accepted the catastrophe as
accidental. "You'd better come up," they said,
"come up and see what you've done." So I went
up, still carrying the sleeping boy.

We emerged into the upper country, but both
the princess and the lake had vanished, for there
was only a broad green meadow, in the middle of
which was a long, low building of stone, very
simple in design, and reminding me in some ways
of a Greek temple. A further band of young men
here joined our group, one of them wearing a
wreath of corn on his head—not wound round it,
but with the blades of corn standing straight up.
He it was who entered the building first, but
immediately he came out again, tearing off his
wreath and throwing it away before he rejoined
us.

Now we all entered, and I found myself in a
large room like a lecture hall. A semi-circular
amphitheatre faced a stage or platform whereon

stood a reading-desk and a tall un-upholstered chair with arms and a straight back. All round the amphitheatre ran stone benches, rising gradually in tiers. The second group of young men seated themselves at the side near the door, the original group still surrounded me, and among them I sat down, directly opposite the desk. "Stay with us," they urged, having become extremely friendly. "He doesn't know; and you can sit on the ground where he won't see you."

So I sat on the ground, and they placed themselves so as to hide me, but I found that from this position I myself could see very little of what was going on. One of them bent down and whispered expectantly, "When he comes, are you going to do anything?"

"When who comes?" I asked.

"The Master. He's coming now."

I tried to peer between legs, but could only make out that somebody had entered and had taken the chair before the reading-desk. There he remained in silence while, one by one, the band of young men seated near the door rose and passed before him, each, as he reached the desk, pausing for a moment and bowing.

My young men did not move, and I had the feeling that something was in preparation, that I was expected by all these youths who were now hiding me to oppose the Master when the moment for an active demonstration should be reached, and that it was for this purpose I had been brought

there. I had been adopted as representing their
cause, and clearly a rebellion of some nature was
on foot, of which neither the Master nor the
young men who had bowed to him at present
knew anything. There was a silence, broken at
last by the sound of a chair being pushed back.
The seated figure, of whom I still had caught only
a glimpse of a pale-coloured robe, must have
risen to his feet—and with that unfortunately I
awoke.

Now this, I can hardly explain why, was from
beginning to end an extremely happy dream. I had
the feeling, in the latter part of it, that all around
me there was an atmosphere of trust and affection,
though how it was conveyed I cannot precisely
say, for I have omitted nothing, and it will be seen
that the whole thing was more or less enacted
in dumb show, was a kind of pantomime in which
the minimum of words was used, all the rest being
conveyed by a sort of telepathic communication
that indeed never ceased. The actual beauty of the
opening scene—the morning and the green landscape, the bright air and the floating boy—was
extraordinary. It was like the fantastic opening
of some tale in *The Arabian Nights*, but with
nothing of the exotic Arabian colouring. As a
story, however, it is full of loose ends. The sleeping boy remained through it from start to
finish. I was still holding him, and he was still
asleep when I woke up. Would he have awakened
at the sound of the Master's voice had the dream

continued? What actually had he to do with it all?
He was important, or he would have vanished
like the princess. But who was the princess and
why had she been drowned? Who was the Master
and for what reason did his pupils wish to defy
him? In fact, "though the words are plain, yet the
thing is obscure—like the finding of the Body of
Moses". The dream collaborator had not settled
these points. It seems unlikely that he ever could
have settled them; he had wandered too far.

So this chapter ended, but since reading it over
and typing it I have had a dream in which a
prolonged time experience does, in a sense, seem
to have been produced almost instantaneously.
What I mean is that, though the action took place
entirely in the present, yet it was powerfully influenced and emotionally coloured by a past that
had taken place before the dream began.

I was wandering in a country I have never
visited in reality—somewhere in North America,
I should imagine, for it was a country of great
plains and rivers and forests, and the ice on the
rivers had only recently melted after a long winter. My age, I suppose, was about twelve or
thirteen, and I was looking for another boy who
had disappeared from home, leaving no message
or clue of any kind. This had happened some
time ago, and the general belief was that he had
been drowned while bathing in the river, and that
his body had been caught among the weeds and

rocks at the bottom. With the melting of the ice I thought it might have been released, and I made inquiries as I pursued my search, but to no purpose. More and more despondent, I still persisted. He might *not* be drowned; he might have gone away; somebody might have seen him; but nobody had. At that moment I saw a large van, like a furniture van, but without a roof, approaching across the empty plain, drawn by four sturdy horses. Evidently it had come from a long distance, and when it drew level with me I boarded it as a last chance. Besides the driver, it contained two or three men lolling and smoking, but I paid little attention to any of these, for there, leaning back amongst some sacking at the side of the van, was the boy I had been searching for, hardly expecting to find him alive. Yet he was alive; there was no doubt of that. These men had discovered him, lost and exhausted, miles and miles from his home, to which they were bringing him back. Obviously he had been ill, for he still looked very white—a small boy with black hair, and wearing a much-patched old blue suit with short trousers. That he was quite convalescent and not greatly perturbed his first words showed: for all he said, as he made room for me beside him, was, "Where you bin, Scummy?"

"I bin lookin' for you for mor'n a year," I answered, suddenly overwhelmed by a passion of relief that reduced me to tears. And this emotion was still in full swing when I awoke.

Now there are several odd points to be noted here. I, apparently, was "Scummy"—a nickname I had not till then heard. The lost boy was not one I had ever known in actual life, yet in the dream we had long been close friends. Still stranger, I was incapable of a more educated speech than that I have tried to indicate phonetically, and which seems vaguely American. The whole dream cannot have lasted longer than the three or four minutes of its climax, yet in that space the deepest affection had found time to spring up, with all the intimate associations of a long companionship behind it.

In a way, of course, the dream is in character. I mean, as a small boy I was quite like Scummy, except that I spoke differently. In fact, two forces appear to have been at work—that of nature, which accounts for everything in connection with poor Scummy (the unflattering name, even, surely is a direct throw-back to the psychology of boyhood), and that of the story-teller of later development, who presented both boys, more or less objectively, as boys of the unlettered class. But how curiously alert is this unawakened story-teller! The men in the van, for instance, were of no importance in the dream; they were scarcely noted, as I have said; yet they were completely realized. Character, appearance, earth-stained clothing, talk—I could do them now in every detail, and the plodding horses, and the landscape, if I were writing the tale as a tale. Moreover, it is the kind of tale I *might* write: it drops more or less into the category of the later tales I *did* write: it could be taken as a suggestion, a prompting; but perhaps this aspect will become clearer in the next chapter.

XVIII

THERE are two flights of stone steps, flanked
by smooth grass banks, leading down to the
fountain in its circular pool. The low balustrades
of the steps are covered with a thick tangled
matting of wistaria, and on an island in the middle
of a shallow stone-rimmed pool there is a small
naked boy holding an urn tilted forward, through
which, when the fountain is playing, the water
gushes. Beside this stone boy crouches a stone
otter, and on his other side stands a stone owl;
while all round the edge of his pool are rough
grey boulders coated with moss, rock plants, and
grasses, among which rise bushes of lavender,
cotoneaster, and barberry. The flat glossy leaves
of waterlilies float on the surface of the pool, and
there are frogs, I know, beneath the dark shelter-
ing leaves. It is, or was, a lovely spot, and always
a favourite one of mine. Seated on those steps,
watched by boy and owl and otter, with Roger,
the sheepdog, drowsing beside me, I wrote a
good deal of *Uncle Stephen*. Now and then a
crimson, spotted ladybird would run across the
white page I had completed; now and then
"frog peeped out o' the fountain"; but there
was no other interruption. So the pool and the
stone boy and the otter and the owl all naturally
found their way into the tale; but Tom and
Uncle Stephen and every other character in it—

except perhaps poor Uncle Horace—came out of dreamland.

Below the fountain and the low fence of rambler roses the ground drops steeply to a valley of meadow-land; then it rises again on the far side of a stream, and the summit of this hill is crowned by a line of trees. The valley is steeped in sunlight, and the line of trees almost, but not quite, shuts out a range of blue mountains beyond, with the lough beneath them. In the hollow on the right lies a tree-shadowed pond where the dogs Roger and Barker liked to swim, carefully avoiding each other, for their relation was one of mutual toleration rather than of friendship. Behind me is the house itself, facing two croquet lawns now knee-deep in unmown grass. On the left is a mound, topped by a grey crumbling ruin that has been transformed into a fernery.

The house is The Moat, and when Frank Workman, who owned it, was alive, I used to play croquet here on most afternoons in spring, summer, and autumn. After his death Mrs. Workman took a dislike to the place, and left it, taking my stone boy with her. I was sorry then that I had ever mentioned him, for nobody had particularly noticed his charm until I had expatiated upon it. And a great deal of his charm was that he fitted so perfectly into his surroundings and into my imagination: in his new surroundings it vanished. Not that it matters any longer, he has become a spirit, and his old surroundings likewise have gone. For twenty years I was familiar with this place; I had become as attached to it as a cat. To-day the house has been turned into flats, the grounds are spoiled, and on my last visit I was warned off as a trespasser by a guardian who knew me not. *Sic transit gloria mundi*—a mere phrase in childhood and youth, but later expressing only too convincing a reality.

Yet The Moat itself does not come into *Uncle Stephen*: two distant places do—the graveyard at Inch Abbey, and the house at Burrenwood, near Newcastle, County Down. I cannot remember who first took me to Inch, but it was with Richard Rowley and Paul Henry that I first visited Burrenwood. That empty house produced an instantaneous and very vivid impression upon me—much the impression that Tom receives in the story, though I altered its surroundings slightly when I was writing about it, bringing in my fountain and my stone boy, altering him, too, a little.

Uncle Stephen in its first form was really and completely a dream story. That is to say, from beginning to end, it was composed in sleep—or perhaps I should say "lived", for I undoubtedly was Tom. Of the exact date of this dream I have no note, but next morning I wrote it all out and sent a summary of it, in the form of a letter, to Walter de la Mare. The first date I have is attached to *his* letter—16th November, 1928—but it is unlikely that more than a few days separated our communications. "Has the magician come on any further?" he asks. "What you said in your letter should be a vivifying nucleus; and though a wicked magician would be easier, a good one would be far more original, and offer a more delicate scope. Have you put anything on paper yet?"

Of course it must have been the barest skeleton of the story—with nothing of its meaning—that I gave him. The goodness of the magician, of Uncle Stephen, was an essential part of the conception, but beyond this I appear to have sketched the meagrest outline, since actually, when he came to read the book, he found it not in the least like what he had expected.

I had simply adumbrated a story of magic and mystery. "*My* Uncle's a Magician" was the original title, with a slight accentuation of the "My", to indicate a small boy's natural pride of possession. That irrational impulse which has always led me to destroy early drafts is here annoying, for I worked over the thing so much that it is impossible now with any certainty to separate the true dream from the novel that grew out of it. This much I can say, that the dream had all the romantic trappings of a tale of magic. In it Uncle Stephen projected a message to Tom, who came at his call (though he cannot then have been named Tom, for in dreams we do not change our names). He knew Uncle Stephen was a magician: the elements of mingled trepidation and curiosity had been implanted in him before he ever left home; and even after he had been welcomed and was living in the house, he was at once fascinated by and afraid to pass the door of Uncle Stephen's private room. There were secret passages (things I had always loved), and beneath the house was a vast stone vault or temple, and in that temple, on a kind of throne, was the black marble beast, the crouching sleeping beast of *Apostate*. All this dates back to the earliest imaginations of childhood—to the days between Emma and school. Then one night the boy was awakened by a sound downstairs, and guessed that a burglar (Deverell, though not the Deverell I later imagined) had broken into the house. He hung over the banisters listening. To reach Uncle Stephen's room and warn him, he had to go down a flight of stairs and along passages. Very nervously he went, his fear increasing as he hovered outside the mysterious and dreaded door. But he screwed up his courage, knocked, went in, and immediately all his fear vanished. For he found himself not in a strange and daunting chamber where the black arts might be practised, but in a room simple and bare as a hermit's cell.

In the dream it was by magic and down in the subterranean temple that Uncle Stephen changed himself back into the boy Stephen; while all the subsequent adventure was complicated by the burning of the house, which prevented him from returning thither and resuming his natural shape.

Now this story was the story I first wrote, and as soon as I had written it I knew it to be wrong. It was wrong because it was melodramatic, and while following the pattern of the dream, entirely missed its spirit. I saw that by changing certain of the incidents—which after all were purely external, and like the subterranean temple clearly belonged to an earlier stage of imaginative activity—I could bring it much nearer to the dream spirit. But by this time dream and waking invention had become hopelessly entangled, so I abandoned the dream entirely, took out the burning of the house and all the magic, introduced Deverell as a character (he had before been only a nameless burglar who never actually appeared on the scene), and began to rewrite the whole thing as realistically as the nature of its content would permit.

With the result, however, that I had now lost the dream explanation—fantastic, of course, but in a sense logical—of the physical metamorphosis. The difficulty seemed insurmountable. I can remember discussing it in the garden at Taplow, and de la Mare making suggestions, only next moment to reject them, so that I saw he thought a solution to be impossible. I thought so too, and was within an ace of abandoning the whole thing. Yet, I don't know why, I had no sooner returned home to Ireland than all we had been bothering about struck me as really of no importance. It was, I now felt, irrelevant; the real story remained precisely what it had been all along—a story of sacred and profane love—the machinery being merely a way of *telling* it. Viewed in this new light, its inner truth was as little affected by external improbabilities as were Socrates' tales of Egypt. What was real was the emotion of which the story was the symbol. The imagination of Tom was the focus, and Tom was absolutely real, even if a rather special little boy, who "felt through all this earthly dress bright shoots of everlastingness".

The relief this brought me was extraordinary. It had been created as if by a whisper in my ear, and I attributed it to my tutelary spirit. So I wrote the dedication to Hermes, and later suppressed it because of the weakness that dreads ridicule. Instead, I prefaced the story with some lines from Wordsworth's *Michael*, and so far as I know only one reader noticed that these lines are repeated in the penultimate paragraph, with merely one or two verbal changes made to bring the verse rhythm into my own prose rhythm.

I loved writing this book, and I wrote it slowly —I might almost say luxuriously. During the two years spent on it Tom grew to be extraordinarily real to me—real, I think, in a way none of my other characters has ever been, so that sometimes for a few minutes I would stop writing because he seemed to be actually there in the room. I knew the tones of his voice, I caught glimpses of him in the street, and one evening, after finishing a chapter, I put down my work to go out for a walk with him.

All this eventually produced a state of mind in which I could have believed nearly anything. It was less like writing a book than living in one. I had the feeling that either Tom was passing out of the spiritual world to come to me, or that I was going to him. Ever more slowly I put my final touches to the story, for I knew that once I had written the last words the spell would be broken, and that I should never be able to recapture it.

XIX

THE PEAR TREE

YOUR hands were not made, I think, for
    picking and stealing,
Or plucking the strings of a fiddle or mending a
    clock.
But to hold in their grasp and to shake the boughs
    of a pear tree,
While I stand below,
And you look down at me, laughing and calling
    through the green leaves.

To the damp long tangled grass the pears drop
    down;
The branches sway and sweep in the air with a
    noise like the rushing of wind.
Soft little thuds on the grass, and your voice from
    the tree top:
"How many? Two? Three? Any luck: any good?"
Old Roger sits patiently watching and hoping for
    sticks.

The pear tree all stripped of its fruit is now silent
    and naked.
Dark and asleep it stands, a grey sky above it.
Clouds are caught in its branches and raindrops
    glisten;
And the bleached winter grass is sodden and
    matted below.

I saw it to-day—a pear tree but not my pear tree.
My pear tree is growing within me: its branches
    are green.
You shake it and call, "How many? One fell close
    by Roger."
And Roger will wait and you laugh and look
    down through the branches
For ever and ever.

XX

FOR *Brian Westby*, the novel I wrote after *Uncle Stephen*, I received no dream prompting, and there is in it no dream element; but the opening of *The Retreat*, its successor, was the exact transcription of a dream. Here I made no change whatever, and the dream ended with the boy (who somehow belonged to an earlier century) coming out into a world of cool green leaves and running water. Starting as a dream of terror, with the entry of the fawn it was abruptly transformed into a dream of happiness, and on waking I saw in this a kind of symbolism, a pledge of the alliance I had formed from the beginning with the animal world.

For a weaver of tales, however, the immediate problem was how to make use of this fragment, which I wrote out at once. Now another fragment had been floating for several years at the back of my mind—a scene this time from waking life, that I very much wished to use, because its strangeness and beauty had impressed me deeply. I had been staying for a few days with E. M. F. in his flat in Brunswick Square, and one afternoon he had taken me to a very small park quite close at hand. This park, I suspect, must originally have been part of, or adjoined, a graveyard, for all along one side of it was a broken wall composed of ancient tombstones, and now, at the hour of our visit, seated on each of these tombstones was a cat. The park was deserted, the cats were motionless, and in the stillness and the fading autumn light, the whole picture seemed drenched in a kind of sorcery, which, partly perhaps because I was so little prepared for it, created an immediate response in my imagination.

Not so in that of my companion, who was pleased by the success of his experiment, but at the same time amused by it. His own impression of the scene was that it was "slightly below par". He had brought me there because, knowing me, he had thought I might like it. I was rather startled to find myself known so well: one always imagines a certain inscrutability. But he was right, I *did* like it, I with difficulty tore myself away from it, and not until I had paused before each of the tombstones and exchanged a prolonged silent gaze with its occupant, during which I was invited to come back at midnight, climb the locked gate, and *then* I should see what I should see.

I did not do so; I always lag behind the promised adventure; dump me down in a hole and I am inclined to remain there for ever; but I knew I should not forget the strange experience. It was rather like meeting one's doppelgänger. After all, nobody expects to be confronted suddenly in the flesh with the stuff of his private imaginings. Yet that was the effect, and from these two sources, the earlier reality and the later dream, finally

emerged, though not without some birth-pangs,
The Retreat. Neither source was in itself sufficient;
but in conjunction—and as I say I had to wait
several years before the conjunction took place—
they proved fruitful.

The first step was to ask myself—Who would
have had the dream? The second was—Who
would have encountered the cats? Well, E. M.,
of course, had encountered them, but that was not
the answer I wanted. The pregnant answer to
both questions was "Tom"—Uncle Stephen's
Tom—and that gave me what I sought. Only it
must be Tom, as I promptly realized, at an earlier
stage in his development than I had presented in
Uncle Stephen; Tom, in fact, at a transition period,
when everything that happened to him should be
new and mysterious, and wishes and fears change
unaccountably and involuntarily into realities.

This was excellent, because it gave me the
opportunity to return to Tom, and that, I
imagined, meant that I could not go very far
wrong, and should certainly enjoy myself. I
should be writing, moreover, about the world I
cared for most—when "meadow, grove, and
stream, the earth, and every common sight" had
"the glory and the freshness of a dream".

A daydream this time, for, unlike *Uncle Stephen*,
with the exception of its first chapter *The Retreat*
came in broad daylight, and much of it from real
life. Even the Donizetti air, the "Spirto Gentil",
I myself had sung when I was Tom's age, though

I had not had Tom's advantage of hearing the
Caruso record, the gramophone having come too
late for that. But both Brown and Pascoe had
been, under other names, at school with me. I left
Brown very much as he was, and I made Pascoe a
little more what I should have liked him to be.
Miss Pascoe herself was a partial portrait, and even
the shop of Pascoe's father, the wine merchant,
was none other than Forrester's dark and cool
and richly fascinating shop in Arthur Street.
Some of the magics of Henry, too, were per-
formed under my own eyes, when I was staying
with him and his master, and we had the house to
ourselves—so there is an independent witness to
those antics at least. Yet it was another cat, named
Jacob, a misanthropic and self-centred "person
on business from Persia", without, I should
think, a shred of sentiment for humanity, who
played the piano to me one afternoon when we
were alone together.

The Chrysanthemum incident took place exactly as I have described it. In addition, I got an
excellent "snap" of Chrysanthemum—in appearance the most prehistoric dog I have ever beheld,
with a fringe over his eyes, and a coat so densely
matted that small birds might have been tempted
to build their nests therein. And the Fort, and the
Manor House, and Glenagivney, and Port-a-
Doris—all these were described on the spot. I
admit that many of the incidents were invented,
and the whole of the plot; for there is both a plot

and a moral—Alice's Duchess would have found the latter at once, as indeed did Edward Crankshaw, who wrote a marvellously penetrating criticism of the book, missing nothing, exaggerating nothing.

And this, I am afraid, brings me somewhat abruptly to the end of my notes. They have been growing, I am conscious, more and more like a commentary and less and less like an autobiography as they approach the present; but that, I think, was inevitable, and after all the commentary forms part of the story. Perhaps indeed, in a story such as this, the chief part. For the external happenings, viewed in retrospect, were few and sober enough. The adventure all along lay in the interpretation, and therefore, as it seems to me now, became really most adventurous precisely in those quieter hours

> When the soul seeks to hear; when all is hushed,
> And the heart listens.

January—December, 1939.

243